ABOUT THE AUTHOR

Cherron Inko-Tariah MBE is a former civil servant and has undertaken leadership roles in HR, and various policy and strategic positions across Whitehall, including working directly with Ministers and Permanent Secretaries. During her time in the Civil Service, she received the Deputy Prime Minister's Award for Excellence and was also shortlisted in the Leadership category of the Civil Service Awards.

Cherron is passionate about staff networks and the positive impact they can have in the business. She is an accomplished Chair of staff networks (one to award-winning status) and has facilitated bespoke training to educate members on the benefits of proactive development.

During her career, she has achieved a Postgraduate Diploma in Human Resource Management, and a Masters Degree in Employment Studies and Human Resource Management. She is a member of the Chartered

1

Institute of Personnel and Development (CIPD) and is also a qualified career coach.

In 2011, Cherron received an MBE for her services to HM Government and her work in the local church community with young people.

WHAT PEOPLE ARE SAYING ABOUT THIS BOOK...

"This book is very well written and I find it a really helpful resource."

Evonne Hopwood - Vice-Chair of a staff network in the Civil Service

"I've no doubt this book will help many new and existing staff networks – and their members – to flourish."

Rasheed Ogunlaru - Coach, Speaker, Author

"This book is, quite simply, a MUST read for all those already in, thinking of, or connected to staff networks."

Rob Neil - Diversity Consultant and Facilitator

THE INCREDIBLE POWER OF

POWER OF

STAFF

NETWORKS

A beacon which shines a light on innovation
and creative co-operation cutting across
all levels of an organisation.

Cherron Inko-Tariah MBE

Published by
Filament Publishing Ltd
16, Croydon Road, Waddon, Croydon,
Surrey, CR0 4PA, United Kingdom
Telephone +44 (0)20 8688 2598
Fax +44 (0)20 7183 7186
info@filamentpublishing.com
www.filamentpublishing.com

The right of Cherron Inko-Tariah MBE to be identified as the author
of this work has been asserted by her in accordance with the
Designs and Copyright Act 1988.

ISBN - 978-1-910125-61-8

Printed by IngramSpark

DEDICATION & THANKS

Firstly, I give God thanks for everything.

I dedicate this book to:
Charles, my fantastic husband and best friend
(thank you for your patience, love and prayers),
and to my wonderful family and friends.

Thank you to **Sir Bob Kerslake** for writing the foreword to this book.

My sincere appreciation to those who cheered me on throughout my
journey. In particular, I would like to say a special thank you to:
**Barbara Lindsay MBE, Caroline Williams, Dionne Campbell-Mark,
Lorraine Thomas, Selvin Brown MBE, Sharone Collins,
Tim Pope, Tommy Cloherty** and **Wendy Irwin.**
I am so grateful for your unwavering support, contribution and love.

As you have watered, may you always be watered.

Peace and love.

ACKNOWLEDGEMENTS

I would like to recognise the following for their valuable contribution:

- Beth Clutterbuck, HSBC Holdings PLC

- Ben Conway, Tree of Life

- Claire Herbert, Equality Challenge Unit

- David Onigbanjo, Organisational Development Consultant

- Diane Greenidge, Bank of New York Mellon

- Effenus Henderson, Hender Works Inc.

- Dr Etlyn Kenny, University of Birmingham

- Gary Denton, HSBC Holdings PLC

- Jacqui Gavin, Dept. of Work and Pensions

- Halil Huseyin, Metropolitan Police Service

- Jennifer Smith, Circle Housing Group

- Joe Montgomery

- Julian Hall, Ultrapreneur

- Keith Morss, Sapphire Projects Ltd

- Keith Willacy, www.equality-matters.co.uk

- Kåre Siversten, Scene Change

- Kulvinder Bassi MBE, Dept. for Transport

- Jerome Williams, Dept. Energy and Climate Change
- Larry Reynolds, 21st Century Leader
- Mairi McHaffie, Coaching Squared
- Matthew Parsons, Radius Business
- Morgan Lobb, DiversityJobs.co.uk
- Nitin Kalra, PeopleStrong (India)
- Paul Deemer, NHS Employers
- Perry Noble, New Spring (USA)
- Peter Hall, Employers Network for Equality & Inclusion
- Rakshita Patel, Terrence Higgins Trust
- Rasheed Ogunlaru, www.rasaru.com
- Professor Ray Friedman, Vanderbilt University (USA)
- Rachel Williams, Inclusive Employers
- Richard McKenna, Inclusive Employers
- Rob Neil, Ministry of Justice
- Robert Dart, Royal College of Nursing
- Robert Smid, PwC
- Roianne Nedd, Business in the Community
- Dr Scott Gaule, Manchester Metropolitan University
- Sonia Brown, National Black Women's Network
- Steve Gooding, Dept. for Transport
- Stuart Crabbe, Facebook
- Vanessa Vallely, We are the City

CONTENTS

About the Author...1

Dedication and Thanks...5

Acknowledgements 7

Foreword..11

Words of Support...13

Introduction 15

Chapter 1: Mirror, Mirror on the Wall............................23
- Ten top tips
- Handling a difficult dialogue

Chapter 2: Understanding Staff Networks 27
- What are staff networks?
- Why are they needed?
- How can staff networks help the business?

Chapter 3: Building Successful Staff Networks 43
- Why start a staff network?
- Types of staff network
- What is your pitch?
- How to start a staff network in six steps

Chapter 4: The Members 61
- Motivating members
- Why people don't join staff networks

Chapter 5: Risks and Maladies..**67**
- The pitfalls of staff networks
- Founders' Syndrome and other staff network maladies

Chapter 6: The Game Plan..**75**
- Terms of reference (C.R.Y.S.T.A.L. clear)
- Code of conduct
- Managing internal conflict

Chapter 7: The Team...**85**
- Leading with grace
- Building the core team
- Getting the best from your meeting
- Squad X (the fifth wheel)
- Tips for handling critical people

Chapter 8: Aligning the Staff Network with the Business...............**99**
- Relationship with senior management
- The staff network champion
- Benefits of a good relationship

Chapter 9: Succession Planning...**113**
- What is it?
- Issues surrounding succession planning
- Practical solutions

Chapter 10: Dear Chair...**119**
- Advice from the heart

Conclusion...**125**

Resources..**129**
- Terms of Reference templates
- Sample letter of support for staff networks
- Wall of Inspiration

References...**141**

Further reading..**144**

FOREWORD

Staff networks are a tremendous force for good within any organisation. I know from my personal experience that, notwithstanding all the terrific work that has been done, we still have groups that are still under-represented either in absolute terms or at particular levels.

A really powerful staff network will understand the importance of working collaboratively across the organisation and can set a model way of working for the whole organisation. When staff networks get together to find innovative solutions to systemic problems to help strengthen the organisation, it shines a light on employees at their absolute best.

Diversity is about having people who look at things in a different way and create a safe space to challenge assumptions and provide better ways of working.

It was great working with Cherron while she was Chair of the Black, Asian and Minority Ethnic staff network in DCLG. Her leadership of this group was really helpful to both me personally and the wider Executive Team.

Sir Bob Kerslake
Permanent Secretary

Department for
Communities and
Local Government

WORDS OF SUPPORT

Just as life in modern society can sometimes leave us feeling isolated and unengaged, life in large organisations too often leaves us feeling unacknowledged and devoid of the sense of deep connection that would enable us to give off our best.

Current management thinking advocates diversity of staff composition alongside 'whole-staff' commitment to a unifying purpose as two of the principles that characterise high performance organisations. Where staff members are drawn from increasingly diverse backgrounds, organisations need new and effective tools to acknowledge the various communities of ethnicity or interest that individuals might identify with. Staff networks can be one such tool. They can help to promote innovation, to open powerfully constructive channels of communication and to promote a sense of fairness - especially in organisations over-attached to hierarchy.

This examination of the value of staff networks draws extensively on efforts to release creativity, improve communication and open up a sense of fairness in England's civil service (and other sectors). Just as society's recent understanding of social networking was starting to blossom, the civil service was investing in the creation of staff networks. In a world where trade union membership has declined significantly, staff networks have much to teach us. This book offers us thoughtful reflections about how we might best understand them.

Joe Montgomery CB

INTRODUCTION

Welcome to *The Incredible Power of Staff Networks*.

A member of a staff network once said to me: "*Those who water will always be watered.*"

This is something that has stuck with me and if I'm honest, accurately captures what I have tried to do whenever I become involved with a staff network. If I can support someone, maybe they can go on to support someone else. It becomes a virtuous circle of support rather than a vicious cycle of destruction. I have watched people blossom from the support, leadership and the empowerment that a staff network provides. I have also witnessed staff networks - that start with the best of intentions - drifting into the sea of poor focus, apathy, and lack of vision.

Any successful business, whatever the sector, whatever the marketplace will:

- Want to recruit and retain the most talented people;
- Aim to provide the best service to clients and customers;
- Want to make a positive difference to the business;
- Understand the value in managing and harnessing the potential of an increasingly diverse workforce.

Staff networks, because of their access and insight, can help organisations do all of these things and provide valuable perspectives - making them more important now than ever before. However, they will face more challenge, scrutiny and expectations. In addition, the changing faces of organisations, diverse workforces, and other demands, will make staff networks - and running them professionally – more key.

Therefore, it is crucial that they have foresight, a good foundation, and the right frame of mind. Only then can they be effective and prominent - acting as a real source of support for their members while simultaneously bringing gradual change in an organisation.

Why on earth should someone write a book about staff networks?

Although I had been involved in different staff networks, there was one experience in particular that motivated me to write this book.

In December 2009, I sat patiently in a conference room with members of a staff network listening to the plans and activities for the year ahead. As I sat there, the staff network shared what they were planning to do. They had some events in the pipeline but little else, and the audience appeared content as they didn't really ask any questions nor did they query the lack of developmental opportunities. Everyone seemed quite satisfied with what was being offered.

Everyone but me!

Part of me was slightly annoyed for two reasons:

1. I was aware that the organisation was about to go through a tremendous change in the next 12-18 months. However, if the staff network knew about these changes, there wasn't any evidence to demonstrate this. There was nothing reflected in their work programme that prepared the membership for the arduous road ahead.

2. I could clearly see the potential of the staff network and was concerned that they weren't tapping into it.

Don't get me wrong, I wasn't intentionally criticising or undermining the staff network. I could see that they were trying to improve things, but I felt frustrated. There was one little voice in my head that said perhaps they were doing the best with who they have and the resources at hand, but the other (and much louder) voice in my head was not appeased. The easiest thing would have been to sit on the sidelines and murmur about the lack of foresight of the staff network. But apart from making me feel better, how would that actually help?

I can't explain why but I thought: *"I've got to do something to help this staff network."* I couldn't shake off this sense of destiny. It was as if my previous work with staff networks, experience in the Civil Service and academic knowledge had formed an alliance for such a time as this.

So I approached them with my concerns. I put before them a plan of a few simple things that I felt they could do to refresh and strengthen the staff network (such as align their aims with the Department, hold an awareness raising campaign, create opportunities to raise the profile of members). I provided the reasons and the possible outcomes of taking on my suggestions. I went further to say what I was prepared to do to help them realise this plan. I, along with others, offered to help the staff network. I wish I could say that they welcomed me and all my suggestions with open arms. Actually, that's unfair. They welcomed the suggestions.

However, some viewed me with suspicion. My motives were questioned and assumptions were made about me as a person. I was accused of getting involved to further my own career because, apparently, I saw the staff network as a stepping stone to promotion.

Despite their misgivings, I got involved in leading the staff network because I believed in its potential and purpose. I believed that my skills and experience would benefit the staff network. I knew that with the right vision, the staff network had the ability to achieve great things and improve outcomes for the members. I had to constantly reiterate that I was there for the greater good of the staff network. Personal gain was not my motivation; my aim was to bring a positive change to the membership.

I won't lie to you. It was tough.

I realised that when people feel threatened or challenged, they behave in a way that they wouldn't normally. I couldn't control their behaviour; only my response. But there were times when I would take myself to a quiet corner, throw my hands in the air and question: *"Why are you doing this, Cherron? Why bother? It's just too much hard work."*

Three things helped me to carry on:

1. My faith;

2. Some of the leadership team would rally round to encourage and support me. That was one of the best things from my experience. Gaining new friends and having a strong, supportive, trusted circle;

3. I was also spurred on when members of the staff network would tell me that they got promoted because of a seminar that we did or that they've decided to get some coaching to help them work smarter based on an email that we sent, or simply just to say thank you. Reports like these motivated the leadership team and me to persevere.

Whenever I wanted to give up, I reminded myself about how frustrated I felt at that meeting in December 2009 and considered the words of Harriet Tubman: *"Every great dream begins with a dreamer. Always remember, you have within you the strength, the patience, and the passion to reach for the stars to change the world."*

I finally accepted that improving outcomes for the members was my quest; my mission for the staff network. I may not be able to change the world but I could make a change in the organisation. I was prepared to raise my head above the parapet for a greater purpose. I was clear about the direction of the staff network. It was an opportunity to transform attitudes and make an impact. It was a chance to show that our target group could think strategically, could demonstrate analytical skills and innovation (these were regularly cited as reasons why ethnic minority staff didn't get promotion to middle management positions). I wanted to prove that with a clear plan, energy, passion and a willingness to work smarter and collaboratively, you can make a difference. That a junior status did not determine one's ability in the staff network because grades were parked at the door; and talent and skill were invited in.

The staff network was fortunate to have a supportive Champion in Sir Bob Kerslake (Permanent Secretary). He listened, challenged and took action where necessary. We had an excellent working relationship based on trust and he valued our insight. Through sheer hard work, partnership working, and achievements, our staff network transformed hearts and minds; not just about the target group but about staff networks in general. I watched people who were rather apathetic and laissez-faire about the staff network become the strongest supporters and advocates for our work. I witnessed members, who at one point coasted along with nominal membership, become active ambassadors.

I experienced first-hand the attitudinal change from members, managers and others. The staff network, that was once a dying plant, blossomed into a wonderful bouquet fragrant with ideas, creativity, and action. A pinnacle of our success was when the staff network received a 'Highly Commended' recognition in the Employee Network category at the Race for Opportunity Awards.

One thing I need to emphasise is that this was NOT an easy journey. Sometimes when people do things well, others assume that it's a piece of cake (ha!). My main focus for the staff network was to help members increase their prospects in development, opportunity and promotion within the organisation. We put the members first and that is what drove our success. In the words of the American actor Danny Thomas: *"Success has nothing to do with what you gain in life or accomplish yourself. It's what you do for others."*

I saw the staff network as a lighthouse - a strong structure with a beacon of light guiding vessels at sea. The lighthouse represents hope, safety, and sustenance. Many of our employee group were 'all at sea' and needed support and guidance from the staff network. The great thing about this experience, and my work with other staff networks over the years, is that it has fuelled my passion to see staff networks be the best they can be.

I know that staff networks can play a crucial role in helping organisations deliver on their goals. They can be a constructive force that can help the business appreciate difference and add to its commercial success. However, many lack the know-how and/or the confidence. As part of my quest, I want to help staff networks to fully comprehend their **P.O.W.E.R.**

What do I mean by P.O.W.E.R?

Purpose and potential - what is their aim as a collective voice?
Opportunity - to strengthen the organisation
Wisdom - in working together
Expectations - how to manage these for members and wider organisation
Responsibility - to themselves, their members and community

The Incredible Power of Staff Networks does three things:

- Offers practical insight into how to run an effective and successful staff network.
- Provides understanding behind the philosophy of staff networks.
- Makes the business case for staff networks so that board members, those in HR and anyone involved in the corporate health of an organisation can tap into the powerful resource of their staff networks.

My experience of staff networks has largely been with Black, Asian and Minority Ethnic (BAME) staff networks in the public sector. However, I have liaised with staff networks representing different equality groups in different sectors in the writing of this book. As part of my research, staff network leaders were asked: "*What help/resources do you actually need or want to run your staff network effectively?*" The responses fell into three main areas:

1. **How to start or improve a staff network in a professional way that benefits members and the organisation;**

2. **How to have the right foundation and mindset in place so that the legacy of the staff network is guaranteed;**

3. **How to work with senior management and be strategic, thus influencing policies and processes within the organisation.**

I address these issues and more.

This book is for you whether:

- You're currently leading (or involved with) a staff network;
- Have ambitions to lead one (or get involved); or
- You want to understand how staff networks can help the organisation.

Glossary of terms/phrases used interchangeably throughout:

- *Target group:* employees that your staff network is primarily aimed at.
- *Minority groups/Minorities:* Refers to anyone that is in a minority e.g. protected characteristics as described in the Equality Act 2010. But please note staff networks are not restricted to these groups.
- *Core Group/Management team/Committee:* The leadership team of the staff network (Chair, Vice Chair, communications, etc).
- *Companies, organisations, business*: The employer.

The final thing to say about this book is that it intends to give it to you straight, with love. Enjoy...

CHAPTER ONE:
MIRROR, MIRROR, ON THE WALL...

"Tell the truth, the whole truth and nothing but the truth."

So you want to lead a staff network. If you dream about becoming the staff network leader extraordinaire, there are some realities that you should know from the outset.

1. Consider whether you are the best person to chair a staff network. (Ouch. Take a minute and let that sink in.) This isn't to say that you cannot make a valid contribution, but it is important to understand the qualities and roles required for the success of the staff network. *See chapter 7 for building the core team.*

2. The staff network is a product with a mission that lives beyond the personality of the Chair. Knowing when to let go is critical to the success of the staff network. *See chapter 9 for succession planning.*

3. A staff network leader should ideally have their strategic antenna tuned in to the workplace frequency (or at least know someone who does). *Chapter 8 talks about the importance of a staff network Champion.*

4. Recognise and exploit opportunities to advance the staff network (not just yourself). For example, seize organisational change as an opening to demonstrate the value and resourcefulness of the staff network.

5. Have a vision of where the staff network is going. This is really about asking: "What is the exam question?" *Chapter 2 has some key questions every staff network should ask itself.*

6. You are advised to develop patience, a very thick skin and the ability to take constructive criticism. Try to remain positive - install and switch on a negative filter. *Chapter 7 covers how to handle criticism.*

7. Learn how to play to people's strengths and see their potential (as well as your own). The staff network is a great arena to develop new skills and strengthen existing ones. *Chapter 7 looks at functions and behaviours of a team.*

8. It helps to be secure in who you are and in your beliefs/values - not to be so rigid that it affects collaboration but not to be so compliant that you compromise your integrity. *Read the 'Dear Chair' letter in Chapter 10.*

9. Choose your battles carefully. Conceding does not mean that you're weak. It sometimes means you're strategic too. Develop, and if possible, master the art of handling a 'difficult dialogue' (see following page).

10. Be compassionate and empathetic but it's imperative to have the ability to remove emotion from your decisions. Failure to do so may result in things being taken personally (which could lead to people becoming professional martyrs).

    Let the following quote be your theme song: ***"good leaders do one thing; they prioritise 'us' over 'me'."***

    And there you have it; my top ten tips for successful staff networks. These all fall into the box labelled: "*I wish someone told me this before I got involved in staff networks.*" That is why I think it is important to understand these elements sooner rather than later.

Power Advice: Handling A Difficult Dialogue

Earlier, I mentioned how important it is to master the art of handling a difficult dialogue. Handling a difficult conversation requires skill and empathy, but ultimately, it requires the courage to go ahead and do it. I think staff networks (and Chairs especially) should master the art of holding difficult dialogues simply because the issues that they need to raise and discuss cannot (and should not) be avoided; neither should they be handled poorly. The following tips by Bruna Martinuzzi (Clarion Enterprises Ltd) aim to help you through a difficult dialogue:

Choose the right place to have the conversation: Consider holding the meeting in a neutral place where you can sit adjacent to each other without the desk as a barrier.

Be clear about the issue: To prepare for the conversation, you need to ask yourself two important questions: *"What exactly is the behaviour that is causing the problem?"* and *"What is the impact of that behaviour?"*

Know your objective: What do you want to accomplish with the dialogue? What is the desired outcome? What do you want to have in your hands by the end of the conversation?

Know how to begin: Some people put off having the conversation because they don't know how to start. Being candid is the authentic and respectful approach. Your tone of voice should signal discussion and not inquisition, exploration and not punishment.

Adopt the right mindset: Spend time to reflect on your attitude toward the situation and the person (or people) involved. What are your preconceived notions about it? Your mindset will predetermine your reaction and interpretations of the other person's responses, so it pays to approach such a conversation with the right mindset.

Manage the emotions: We need to manage and understand the emotions in the discussion. Be mindful of preserving the person's dignity – and treating them with respect – even if we totally disagree with them.

Be comfortable with silence: There will be moments in the conversation where there is silence. Resist the urge to fill it with words. The periodic silence in the conversation allows us to hear what was said and lets the message sink in. A pause also has a calming effect and can help us connect better *(please note that this is different from someone using silence to thwart the discussion).*

Be aware of thwarting ploys: Lying, threatening, stonewalling, crying, sarcasm, shouting, accusing, taking offence: tough talks can present an arsenal of thwarting ploys. But you also have an array of potential responses, ranging from passive to aggressive. The most effective is to move to the middle: disarm the ploy by addressing it. For instance, if your counterpart has stopped responding to you, you can simply say, *"I'm not sure how to interpret your silence."*

Save the relationship: Be mindful to limit any damage to a relationship. Think about how the dialogue can fix the situation, without erecting an irreparable wall between you and the person.

Way forward: End the discussion with clearly expressed action items. What is the person agreeing to do? What support are you committed to provide? What obstacles might prevent these remedial actions from taking place? What do you both agree to do to overcome potential obstacles? Schedule a follow-up to evaluate progress and definitively reach closure on the issue at hand.

CHAPTER TWO:
UNDERSTANDING STAFF NETWORKS

"Diversity is what you see; inclusion is what you feel."
(Stuart Crabbe, Head of Learning, Facebook)

This chapter looks at the composition of staff networks and explores why they are needed as much today as they were when they started in the 1970s.

Staff networks by their very nature are about change. In fact, they are critical agents of change. They exist largely because there is a desire to see a difference in an organisation. But there is confusion about what they are and what they do. There isn't a governing body for staff networks nor are there a set of rules about how they should operate. Therefore, what we have is a range of competing approaches that create ambiguity. Questions about the role of staff networks include:

1. What are they really for?

2. Who do they exist to serve?

3. Are they ineffective talking shops where disgruntled members of staff (from certain groups) gather to have a good moan about their experiences in the workplace?

4. Are they an extension of the trade union?

5. Or are they a way of providing opportunities for members to achieve?

Staff networks have been an unknown entity that many, especially those in management, have found difficult, even if they are willing, to understand. In fact, some managers view staff networks as divisive and contradictory and ask: *"How can network groups try to enhance integration through a strategy of occasional separation?"* (John Brown Childs, Sociologist) Good question.

Beth Clutterbuck, Global Head of Organisational Development (HSBC Bank), says: *"Society is uncomfortable with difference; organisations are often uncomfortable with difference. Employee networks, by their very nature, typify difference. But by supporting these communities and embracing different perspectives, organisations can realise benefits for colleagues and customers."*

Power Thought

Not all networks are seen in a negative light, are they? Let us not forget about those networks that are just automatically accepted and have been for years. Networks like the 'Old Boys Network', 'Old School Tie Network' or fraternities/sororities? Members have a similar background, education, and are provided with a gateway to a variety of advantages and connections both in their careers and social activities. *They* are not seen as divisive and are not open to everyone - only the select few. And yet, these networks are accepted - no questions asked.

What are they and why do they exist?

Staff networks have been described as:

> *"Cooperative structures where an interconnected group or system coalesce around a shared purpose and where members act as peers on the basis of exchange and reciprocity, based on trust, respect, and mutuality"*

(Health Foundation)

"They bring together people who identify with a minority group and/or have an interest in matters relating to the diversity strands (i.e. gender, sexual orientation, race, religion, age and disability)"

(Dr Scott Gaule, Manchester Metropolitan University)

Staff networks are mini-communities, and the old adage 'Strength in Unity' comes to the fore when attempting to describe the essence of good staff networks. Also known as employee affinity groups, employee support or resource groups, diversity groups, staff networks endeavour to *"foster smaller, stronger communities within the larger organisation to provide support and connections."* (Ray Friedman, Professor of Management, Vanderbilt University)

Why?

Research by Herminia Ibarra (Professor of Organisational Behaviour, Insead Business School) found that people from particular minority groups, may not have as many "close ties" at work as their majority counterparts, making it less likely that they receive social support and mentoring. So staff networks through meetings, group volunteering, talks with upper management, and training sessions, provide employees with opportunities *"to meet and develop relationships to expand their networks"* (Friedman).

Effective staff networks engender both social support and career optimism for minorities. Just as skills and abilities are indispensable to success, so too are corporate social relations and ties important for professional growth, development and advancement.

This chimes with the theory which suggests that people are more likely to create ties with people who they deem to be similar. In colloquial terms, "birds of a feather flock together." Social network theorists call this 'homophily' (the tendency of individuals to associate with others of the same kind). Given that many staff networks are comprised of members who share a common social tie or social identity (gender, ethnicity, faith, grade etc), there is some credence in the 'homophily' theory. It makes sense that a numerical minority would come together. But it can't just be about congregating in the workplace with a group of people who look like each other or have something in common. That's what lunchtimes are for! There has to be a desire for something more; to change something, to alter the status quo - otherwise, why the need for support?

When employees fail to feel benefits of genuine inclusion from their employer, they have two options. They can leave, taking their talent, knowledge and expertise with them, or as a preferable alternative, remain in the organisation and seek support from those who can offer empathy (i.e. a staff network) and hopefully help identify a way to manage or move forward.

Staff networks are also started because there is a perception that some members of staff are adversely affected by the processes, procedures, culture or something else, in the business.

Why should we care?

Over the last 50 years, equality legislation necessitates that employers...

"...are proactive in promoting equality of opportunity for all staff as well as consulting and involving staff (and other stakeholders) in the development and implementation of strategies designed to eliminate discrimination and promote equality of opportunity." (Gaule)

Power Insight: Defining Equality, Diversity and Inclusion

Equality is about creating a fairer society where everyone can participate and has the same opportunity to fulfil their potential. Equality is backed by legislation (Equality Act 2010) designed to address unfair discrimination, harassment and victimisation; advance equality of opportunity and foster good relations between people who share a protected characteristic and those who do not. There are nine protected characteristics: age, disability, gender reassignment, marriage and civil partnership, pregnancy and maternity, race, religion and belief, sex, sexual orientation.

> **Diversity** acknowledges and values the full range of differences between people both in the workplace and in wider society. Diversity acknowledges that entry into the workplace and an individual realising their potential once there can be influenced by a range of factors beyond the characteristics included within equality legislation, including social, economic and educational background, professional background, hierarchical level, working style, nationality etc.
>
> **Inclusion** refers to an individual's experience within the workplace and in wider society and the extent to which they feel valued and included.
>
> *Equality, Diversity and Inclusion Strategy 2012-2015, Department for Energy and Climate Change (2012)*

It is fair to say that there has been a gradual shift in focus from equal opportunities, which centred on the right to be treated without discrimination, to diversity which encouraged organisations to encompass uniqueness, acceptance and respect, to inclusion. Inclusion is a systematic strategy that seeks to ensure that all members within the organisation have:

"a voice that is heard, access to the information necessary for success, productive links to other co-workers and management, the chance to contribute, and the opportunity to advance professionally"

(Priscilla H Douglas, Executive Coach)

That is exactly what staff networks aim to do. To be a collective voice that articulates what those perceived issues are and highlight that, for a multitude of reasons, not all employees have access to a level playing field and this, in the long run, can affect the 'bottom line'.

An organisation's success and competitiveness depends not only on its ability to embrace diversity, but that diversity found in the business is reflected in the make-up of the workforce (at all levels) and the provision of services.

Diversity specialists Subeliani and Tsogas suggest that increased diversity can lead to a better understanding of local markets and customers, increased ability to attract and retain the best people, greater creativity, better problem solving and greater flexibility for organisations. Staff networks are unique because they can bring people together who have a common purpose to change their environment and help the business remain competitive. Therein lies some of their power. Gaule says:

"The development of staff networks is recognition of the fact that people come together in many different ways and that they can contribute to development of policies and working practices...staff networks can open the door to changing the culture of the organisation."

Employers will honestly believe that they advocate diversity and inclusion. But in reality, this sometimes means that they are doing what they need to do in order to meet targets or legal requirements (ticking that box). Some employers understand the value and the business case for diversity, but instead of finding a systemic solution to a systemic problem, they tend to employ lots of different initiatives aimed at particular groups. This could explain why, in spite of the great strides made in equality legislation, and spend on diversity/inclusion training in the UK, the 'playing fields' in organisations still aren't level for everyone.

Staff networks can point out the chasm between the rhetoric of the equal opportunities policy and diversity commitment of the organisation, and the reality. Successful staff networks can take it one step further and help the business close the gap, venture to even out the playing field and strive for equity (not just equality).

Because they encourage employees to share their social identity at work, staff networks enable minority groups to foster an authentic and empathetic environment in which co-workers may challenge existing social arrangements and come to *"imaginatively identify with the states of others"* (Dr Neil Fligstein, Berkeley University).

In other words, staff networks help the business develop 'Organisational Empathy'; guiding employers to recognise and begin to understand what some staff members (and external stakeholders) are experiencing. In her book, *To Kill a Mockingbird*, Harper Lee wrote "...*you never really understand a person until you consider things from his point of view...until you climb inside his skin and walk around in it*". In a sense, the purpose of staff networks is to do just this; to shine a light on the negative experiences faced by members with an aim to help the business understand what it is like to work in that environment from the perspective of their members; to climb into their skin. Their collective intelligence enables staff networks to function as effective consultative and advisory bodies on diversity and business related matters.

"Understanding our diverse client base is central to our success. Therefore, we aim to form diverse teams of employees with a wide range of backgrounds and points of view. It is this diverse workforce which will help us attract and retain top talent for the company and enable us to develop innovative product and services as well as maintain our competitive edge."

(Rhonda Mimms, President of ING Foundation)

The beauty of successful staff networks is that when they act as an effective conduit between their members and the wider organisation, they can make great strides in levelling the playing field and tackling other corporate issues.

Case Study: Positive Support Group (PSG), Department for Transport (DfT)

When a number of their members shared concern surrounding the protocols for interview panels, PSG decided to investigate. They uncovered a wealth of anecdotal evidence to indicate that some line managers were approaching friends to assist them on interview panels. This raised issues around the impartiality and the fairness of all interview panels being held within DfT. At the time, the only safeguard was that the line manager was requested to choose someone from outside their immediate directorate to serve on their panels. This, however, did not prevent some from using friends to help them appoint their preferred candidate regardless of whether there was someone more suitable for the post. The staff network wanted to improve the current system through a procedural change to ensure impartiality and suggested taking the process of appointing a Chair out of the hands of the advertising line manager, and instead giving it to the HR Recruitment Team. Working in partnership with HR, the PSG assisted in the development of the "Independent Chair" system. Under the new system, HR randomly appoints the Chair for all interview panels. Furthermore, the Chair has responsibility for ensuring that no unnecessary barriers have been placed by the line manager by vetting the essential criteria for the job advert ahead of publication. PSG Chair says: *"An important role for staff networks in discharging their critical friend role is drawing a light to questionable working practices."*

(Kulvinder Bassi MBE)

As an additional bonus, the corporate health of the whole business is greatly improved. The savvy employers get this. They will acknowledge and support the culturally diverse realities of their people, and harness these experiences in order to develop more inclusive and cohesive cultures. This logic makes for a compelling business case, because if a business is working in the dark and doesn't know how people from different identity groups experience the workplace, how can it really know that what they're doing is appropriate, accessible and inclusive?

Effective staff networks, through their 'intrapreneurship', can help switch the light on. It makes sense that if companies want to access the best talent pool, and have a competitive advantage, then a concerted effort to increase knowledge and gain a better understanding of multicultural, global customers is vital. Staff networks, through the experience and knowledge of their members and communities, can help them in this quest.

Organisational behaviour theorist Dr. Alison Konrad says that diversity *"unleashes creativity, innovation, and improved group problem solving."*

Power Thought: How much does the UK spend on equality and diversity training?

Trick question. It's nigh on impossible to answer this question purely from a cost aspect. Perhaps the question should be "What is the case for equality and diversity?" This should be viewed from three angles, says Keith Willacy (www.equality-matters.co.uk).  *"The social case (because it's the right thing to do, the legal case (because we must do it as per equality legislation etc.), and then the business case (showing the business advantage that we can get from embracing equality and diversity). Once all three angles are embraced and adopted, everything else should fall into place."*

How can staff networks help the business?

Power is shifting based on the huge demographic changes occurring around the world. Effenus Henderson *(CEO and President of Hender Works Inc)* says:

> *"The organisations that understand, embrace, and value change will be more agile, flexible and able to adapt to the changing world. Leaders must embrace staff networks as important components of a comprehensive, forward-looking organisational strategy. In a sense, by building more inclusive processes and systems, more sustainable enterprises will be created."*

Recent figures by Diversity Jobs UK show that:

- By 2020, 20% of the UK's population will be of ethnic origin.
- 40% of LGBTQ staff feel uncomfortable coming out to their employer.

- UK ethnic groups have a spending power of £300 billion per year.
- There are over 80 million people with a disability across the EU.
- 75% of FTSE 100 companies have inaccessible career websites.

Employers cannot assume that just because there are opportunities in the organisation, recruits will see them as their employer of choice. It is important to promote an inclusive culture within the workplace but this...

"...requires a commitment from the top to trigger a change in culture and attitude... employee representatives (staff networks) can play their part in facilitating an evolution in working practices by offering advice and support to employees."

(Talent not Tokenism, Confederation of Business Industry)

Morgan Lobb, CEO of Diversity Jobs UK says: *"Brands (employers) failing to address internal diversity by not laying down a solid foundation risk creating a workforce culture alienated from society, the knock-on effect will be that you are missing valuable talent and the richness a multicultural/diverse staff base will bring."*

Power Thought

Discrimination (be it conscious or unconscious) is illegal and needs to be eliminated. Three key steps towards elimination:

1. The willingness to accept that it exists;

2. The determination to understand both the **composition** *and* the **impact** of discrimination; and

3. The commitment to learn how to effectively challenge it.

Through their collective intelligence, staff networks can provide insight into the experiences faced by their members. They can draw on the skills and understanding of their target group to help employers have a strategy to manage and harness the potential of an increasingly diverse workforce. Staff should have appropriate role models with whom they can identify, and have access to services that are sensitive to and reflect different cultural realities.

Power Insight: Microaggressions 101 (Thamina Jaferi, Turner Consulting Group)

Microaggressions are those subtle slights that occur daily for so many people from diverse communities, backgrounds, and identities. The slights can be hard to identify or "prove". Yet the affected people know they exist because of how these microaggressions make them feel. Although these acts are not as noticeable to others in the same way that blatant "in your face" discrimination is, their cumulative effect can often be just as damaging to the target, and arguably more damaging. The term microaggression can be used to describe slights directed towards marginalised groups on the basis of race, disability, faith, sexual identity, gender identity, and citizenship status, among other characteristics. People are more prone to encounter this type of discrimination as they can often be viewed as harmless interpersonal exchanges (banter) despite their damaging effects on employee self-esteem and morale. Because they can go undetected, microaggressions can impact the workplace profoundly. It is well known that bias (whether conscious or unconscious) can underlie workplace interactions in a subtle way and can have an impact on the health and well-being of employees. As a result, this can negatively affect the employer's own objectives and operations. It is important for employers to turn their minds towards dealing with microaggressions in order to ensure that they are providing a healthy and productive work environment for everyone. **Staff networks** can help point out what these look like in the organisation and identify proactive measures including:

- **Training** to increase awareness about microaggressions. These issues are not necessarily covered in organisational discrimination and harassment policies, and can often be overlooked as a result.

- **Create safe and respectful spaces** to discuss microaggressions that people from diverse communities, backgrounds, and identities face. Everyone in the workplace should be open to dialogue, learning, and ensuring people are not penalised in any way for bringing awareness to these issues. Innovative ways of creating these safe spaces should be explored, such as the use of technology and social media.

- **Develop a set of microaffirmations** for managers to use e.g. small appreciative gestures like a smile or a nod that acknowledge the worth of employees as individuals.

For more information, go to:
http://turnerconsultinggroup.weebly.com/blog-thamina-jaferi

Case Study: Jennifer Smith, Group Head of Diversity at Circle Housing

I felt that there was a place for diversity networks and a role to play in driving the business on. I researched extensively how other diversity networks were established and looked at models and Terms of Reference from organisations in the public and private sector. I felt strongly that we needed to ensure the networks were not exclusive but open to all colleagues. I also felt that timing was key in order to ensure the networks were properly understood and valued by the business - not just regarded as talking shops or freewheeling clubs or cliques that didn't really support the diversity or organisational strategy.

Increasingly, new members of staff who join networks are saying that the diversity agenda at Circle influenced their decision to apply to work in the organisation.

What was the business imperative for the networks at Circle?

- To be courageous, creative and inclusive with our diversity agenda.

- To create a new sense of openness and celebration of our diverse workforce.
- To ensure the business owned the staff networks and that the diversity agenda was being driven at all levels, not just from the centre.
- To really understand issues within our workplace culture, a whole new wealth of eyes and ears across different strands of diversity.
- To sense check our diversity strategy and to ensure that the issues and problems we needed to tackle as a business were indeed the right ones that mattered most to colleagues.
- To nurture and develop diverse talent, and be an important element of recruiting from a diverse talent pool.

Staff networks can play a variety of roles:

- Drive change across the organisation;
- Simply unite individuals with common interests;
- Focus on how to commercially impact the business.

Then there are those staff networks that do a combination of all three and collaborate with other 'sister' staff networks in different organisations.

Case Study: The Network of Networks - BAME/ Multicultural Chapter

The Network of Networks (TNON) BAME/Multicultural chapter was established in September 2011. Membership spans a broad range of top FTSE companies and other leading businesses from sectors such as professional services and law firms. It aims to add business value by demonstrating the tangible benefits and positive effects of BAME/multicultural networks to their businesses' bottom line. TNON is less about running events and more about the business of managing networks and enabling network leaders to become a strategically relevant voice within their organisations. *"We believe that when diverse talent takes its rightful place, it enhances the organisation's success. That is why we support our network leaders in driving their agendas and increasing the value they add to their businesses."*

(Diane Greenidge, Deputy Chief Administrative Officer – Europe, BNY Mellon, Co-Founder – The Network of Networks)

"Networks can give you insights that help you to drive your business forward." says Dianah Worman, Diversity Adviser at the CIPD. *"They are a way to help organisations to understand the people who work for them and to help the business perform better."*

Too good to be true? Here are a few examples of what some staff networks have achieved:

- When BT launched its new broadband internet box, members of Able2 (its disability network) trained installation engineers to allow visually impaired customers to feel the box before it was installed.
- At Cisco, the women's network helps business development by hosting events for prospective and existing female customers – it attributed a significant Swiss contract to a contact made at a gathering of the network.
- In Leeds, a member of Innov8 NHS, a network focused on getting more black and ethnic minority staff into leadership roles across Yorkshire and the Humber region, published a report on how mental health services can be improved for ethnic minority patients, who traditionally suffer poorer mental health.
- At Circle Housing, their staff networks (BAME, Carers, Disability, LGBT) have all influenced changes to policies and processes in the organisation. For example, maternity and adoption policies are more inclusive, there is a concerted drive to improve the recruitment process, a new policy to support carers in the workplace has been created, and there have been great strides made in improving and publicising reasonable adjustments.

Power Insight: Staff networks in the health sector

In its review on staff networks, the Health Foundation found that staff networks are growing in number and importance in the UK. They are ideally placed to tackle systemic and complex problems faced by decision-makers, commissioners, providers, and regulators, as well as frontline staff and service users. Among the evidence that does exist, studies have found that networks can improve quality both directly and indirectly. For example, creating cohesive and collaborative professional networks helps coordinate care. By creating social capital among employees, networks can improve performance and job satisfaction while reducing burnout and staff turnover. They may also have a more symbolic impact through publications, events and images that foster network identity and legitimacy. A network's cooperative, collegial environment allows 'bottom up' views to contribute to solving complex planning, design and delivery problems – bridging gaps between professional groups and competing organisations. And a staff network can provide a forum for addressing inconsistent practice and variations in outcomes.

Chapter Summary

As the examples in this chapter demonstrate, when they remain focused, collaborative and have the right leadership, staff networks can be an effective vehicle for all staff and play an integral part in helping to deliver the goals of the business.

They have an important role in helping to safely and constructively challenge the status quo in organisational development. This challenge helps to mitigate gaps in workforce representation and in processes and systems that may unintentionally favour certain groups.

Effective staff networks can provide an avenue to offer support and solutions to some of the barriers employees face in the work place - be they a 50+ white male in a junior grade or a female executive with a disability.

Finally, any successful business, whatever the sector, whatever the marketplace, will:

- Want to recruit and retain the most talented people;
- Aim to provide the best service to clients and customers;
- Want to make a positive difference to the business.

Staff networks can help you do all of these things and provide valuable insight and different perspectives.

CHAPTER THREE:
BUILDING SUCCESSFUL STAFF NETWORKS

"The loftier the building, the deeper must the foundation be laid."
(Thomas à Kempis)

So, we now have an idea of what they are, and an understanding of the rationale behind their existence. This chapter focuses on the first steps to take and how to build a solid foundation for a successful staff network.

Why start a staff network?

Please don't start your answer by saying: *"I'm passionate about the agenda."* Everyone is passionate about something but they don't start a staff network because of it.

Take a moment and think about it. Here's a box for you to jot down some thoughts.

Why do I want to start a staff network?

With the right tools and guidance, your staff network can have a real impact on its members. They can also be a positive influence in the organisation, but a strong foundation is essential.

If a person or a group believes that their feelings, issues, concerns etc. aren't being addressed by those in a position to change things, then they usually see a staff network as the answer. They get together and agree to go and fight the oppression through continuous tub-thumping until they get some sort of concession or assurance that their voice has been heard.

Ultimately, this approach is not sustainable and is perhaps rather risky because those in management start to think: *"Here they go again...making noise about the same thing that only they care about. Just placate them and they'll go away."* The staff network is then seen as an ineffective group with no real voice, making lots of annoying noise. The building blocks of the staff network start to erode under the weight of doubt, accusations, poor planning, hidden agenda, insecurity, fear etc. etc.

OK, perhaps the above example is a little far-fetched, but there are truths to be found here. It is true that many staff networks are started because there is a belief that 'corporate' or 'management' is not addressing particular issues appropriately or sufficiently. They are driven by passion, involve their like-minded friends and invite people to a meeting to discuss the injustice being suffered by their representative group. The person who raised the issue tends to take the position of leadership and those who supported them from the beginning are the core/executive/management team. Sound familiar? So let's start from the beginning.

The right mindset is vital. If you are thinking about starting a staff network or you want to strengthen an existing one, there are two key questions that you should consider:

1. Why should/does the staff network exist?

2. Why are you starting, or involved in, the staff network?

There has to be a fundamental reason for starting or being involved in a staff network that goes beyond personal need, gripe or promotion. For example:

- A common concern about a particular issue;
- Ongoing issues affecting a group of people e.g. promotion (or lack thereof), development, performance management, stagnation, progression; or

- Emerging process or policy that could have an adverse impact on certain members of staff.

The reason some staff networks fail is because there is a problem with their foundation. Emotion, anger and frustration - while valid in their own right - may be strong reasons to start a staff network, but they are insufficient ones to sustain the life of one. Wendy Irwin, writer and expert on inclusion, advises: *"Don't start what you can't sustain."*

There are some staff networks that enjoy having that 'pressure group' status or relish having a reputation of being adversarial but at the end of the day, is this really a viable approach? Whether you like it or not, you are an employee first and foremost. You receive a salary in exchange for work - this is the priority as far as your employers are concerned. Therefore, any attempt to advocate change for a group of people must have the welfare of the organisation in mind. To do that, you need to demonstrate an understanding of what the issues are. To do that, you must be prepared to do some homework and display strategic thinking.

Let's get back to those two questions:

1. Why should/does the staff network exist?

2. Why are you starting, or involved in, the staff network?

Power Extra:

If you're already involved in a staff network, there is a third question to ask: **Does the staff network receive more sneers than cheers?** This question is really about being aware of how the staff network is perceived so that you can, if need be, adjust your strategy and communication accordingly.

However, you may be surprised to hear that there are people involved in staff networks, who avoid these questions like the plague. They somehow think it's obvious why someone engages in a staff network. But the truth is, it isn't obvious because people start or join staff networks for different reasons. However, I have come across staff networks that believe they don't need to define what their staff network does. Newsflash. Actually, you do.

So, here's a task for you:

> **Define the purpose of a staff network (without the aid of an internet search engine):**
>
>
>
>
>

If you found this relatively easy, you get a gold star. ★

However, if you struggled with this, you are not alone. Leaders of staff networks struggle with this. Some say: "*It's always been there...we just get together to sort out different problems.*" Others claim: "*It's our private space to discuss issues faced by our members within the organisation.*"

Statements like these are valid - up to a point. Failure to properly communicate the role and activity of the staff network can be detrimental. A guarded attitude could be the reason why non-members make assumptions about what happens at these 'secret' meetings.

Would you join or support an organisation or staff network without knowledge of who they are or what they do? Likewise, staff networks need to be able to articulate their purpose or face being labelled as an adversarial pressure group, and all the connotations that go along with that. Not good.

Chairs of successful staff networks have different reasons for starting a network and differing experiences, but they are unanimous in the importance of understanding the 'what', 'why' and 'how' of the staff network.

People start or become involved in a staff network because they want to make a difference and see a change. But time and again, their lack of reasoning and consideration for the members leads one to ask the question: "a difference to whom exactly?" There is a great quote by Julian Hall (Ultrapreneur) which captures the mindset that staff network leaders should be looking to adopt: *"Don't look out for number one; look out for everyone."*

If improving outcomes for members is the ultimate goal, then the sky is the limit because you are driven by seeking the best for the staff network. You could think differently. You should think strategically. Strategic thinking is critical. Before making any decision, you will ask yourself: *"How will this benefit the members?"* or *"How does this impact on the business as a whole?"* or *"Is there reputational/commercial risk or gain for the organisation?"*

It may seem like a no-brainer, but this line of thinking is not as common as it should be (common sense is not always common practice). Believe it or not, there are some people who use the staff network to improve their own career chances. Shock horror! What's wrong with that? Nothing as such but if that's all you care about, then this attitude can easily (and usually does) have a harmful effect on the members. It also creates instability and reputational risk for the staff network because, instead of asking: *"How does it benefit members?"* you are constantly thinking: *"How will this benefit me?"*

This line of thought can weaken the foundation. A successful staff network focuses on how it can effectively improve outcomes for its membership and competently help the business achieve its goals.

The following are definitions of the words SUSTAINABLE and EFFECTIVE.

> *...to support... bear the weight of... endure without giving way...*
> *to keep going... to uphold as valid or just... keep in existence...*
> *encourage... to keep up competently...*

...adequate to accomplish a purpose...
producing the intended or expected result...
producing a deep or vivid impression... striking...

Would you really want to be involved in a staff network that couldn't 'support' or was unable to 'accomplish a purpose'? Of course not!

So, if you're starting a staff network, ask yourself some questions. Such as:

- Who is it for? (a specific equality group? anyone?)
- What do you want the staff network to achieve? (ethos/raison d'être)
- What are your goals?
- What is your strategy for achieving your aim/goals?
- What can you bring to the table? (skills, expertise, knowledge etc.)
- How will the organisation and members benefit from your staff network?
- What will you do that's different to what has been done before?
- What resources do you have at your disposal?
- What is your legacy?
- What is the strapline? Do you need a logo?

What would a good staff network NOT look like?

If you already have a staff network and are looking to strengthen the foundation, here are some questions for you:

- Is the staff network missing in action (MIA)? Or is it focused on **M**ission, **I**mpact and **A**ction?
- Is the staff network doing what it originally set out to do?
- Are members and the organisation benefiting from your staff network?
- Are you shouting about these benefits?
- What is your legacy?

> **Evidence to support your answers:**

Type of Staff Network

Something else to consider is, what type of staff network do you want to have? Might seem like a strange question but it's an important one, as this plays a critical role in determining how the staff network progresses. You don't just want to simply tick a box.

Established using the principles of self-organisation, staff networks are usually supported (and sometimes resourced) by the employer. Some are set up in response to different needs and more often than not, assume the role of a "critical friend" to the employer, acting in an advisory capacity, supplementing and supporting traditional staff consultation and representation channels.

Staff networks can take on different forms. For example:

1. They can be informal, with members meeting on a regular basis to share problems and seek solutions;

2. They can take on a more formal role with a Chair, executive committee, objectives, deliverables etc. all geared at influencing organisational policy, processes or practices for the benefit of their members; or

3. They can be virtual – connecting on an ad-hoc basis but sharing information on a regular basis.

In terms of approach, the most effective staff networks adopt a tactic that aims:

i) To bring change and improve career opportunities for its members; and

ii) To demonstrate how its work can help the organisation improve its corporate health, achieve its business goals and/or the community it serves.

"A staff network can provide their members with support and appropriate training, but if individuals perceive that the deck is being stacked against them they are unlikely to realise their full potential."

(Kul Bassi MBE, Staff Network Chair)

The Liverpool Primary Care Trust and the Liverpool Community Health Care NHS advises that staff networks consider their specific purpose. For example:

- Provide a channel for communication between the Senior Management and staff groups who have been traditionally under-represented or who have experienced discrimination within the workplace.
- Maximise the contribution of staff groups in the decision-making processes of the organisation with a view to fulfilling the commitment to the Equality and Diversity agenda.
- Contribute to equality and diversity awareness training of all staff and service users.
- Offer a safe learning environment for members.
- Provide role models and advocates for progress in making diversity happen and work.
- Empower staff by improving their knowledge of local, regional and national issues in health care.
- Provide access to role models to build confidence and inspire individuals.
- Promote the organisation in the wider community as an employer of choice.

What function do you want your staff network to provide?

The core functions of a staff network can vary significantly depending on the purpose and structure of the network.

Research by the Health Foundation found that networks have six main functions:

1. Community building – promoting and sustaining members' values.

2. Filtering – organising and managing relevant information.

3. Amplifying – helping make public and comprehensible, new and little-known or little-understood ideas.

4. Facilitating and learning – helping members carry out activities more effectively and efficiently.

5. Investing and providing – offering members resources to achieve goals.

6. Convening – bringing together people or groups with distinct strategies to support them.

These functions are not unique to staff networks, but thinking about the function of your staff network is a crucial exercise.

Take a look at the organisational and maturity model overleaf.

Where is your staff network on this model?

- Is the staff network **independent**?
- Is the staff network **engaged**?
- Is the staff network **aligned** to the business goals of the organisation?

Staff Networks Organisational Alignment and Maturity Model ©

Independent: Activities run by the staff network in isolation

- Activity driven independently by group
- No formal engagement with organisation

Engaged: Beginning to influence across the organisation

- Senior level support and engagement
- Specific goals set by Staff Network
- Some accountability and recognition of Staff Networks

Aligned: SN aligned to organisational goals

- Organisational and staff network goals aligned
- Chair/role recognised in career development
- Board-level engagement
- Clear focus and targets
- Staff network groups work together
- Internal and external recognition

Model courtesy of Radius Business

It may be that the staff network is at one of the stages or in between two stages, but taking the time to think about this model is important. The staff network might be at the 'independent' stage acting as a social group, and some leaders of staff networks at that stage may be content with this. Be aware that questions may arise about the longevity and legacy of a staff network remaining at this stage. To make a real impact in the organisation, and sustain that impact, shouldn't staff networks evolve to the "engaged" or "alignment" stage?

Questions to consider:

- Do you know your organisation's business strategy? What are their goals? If not, how will you find out?
- How relevant are these goals to your staff network?
- What are the three things that your staff network may need to respond to as a result?

What are your answers?

The form and approach is entirely up to the staff network but it is vital to understand how the network will operate and how it will be perceived (not to do so would be naïve).

What is your pitch?

Another way to think about the foundation of your staff network is how would you 'pitch' it to a potential member or a sponsor? In the BBC television programme *Dragon's Den*, entrepreneurs pitch their ideas in the hope of securing financial support from the panel of business investors. As part of their pitch, they must demonstrate a thorough understanding of their product.

All staff networks should consider adopting a similar approach.

- What is the problem you are trying to solve?
- What is your product/service? What are you offering?
- Who are your customers?
- What is your USP (unique selling point)?
- How will you measure success/impact?
- What resources do you need and how can you demonstrate added value?

Taking the time to deliberately go through these types of questions and issues strengthens the foundation of the staff network. In addition, having a powerful narrative or "lines to take" about the staff network makes it easier when communicating and publicising to members, potential members, wider organisation etc. about who you are and what you do. It's almost emulating the Disneyland philosophy. No matter which member of staff you encounter at Disney, they are dedicated to the company's mission. Everyone in a staff network should know and be committed to the mission.

Power Test

You get into the lift and the only person in there is your CEO/ Permanent Secretary/Managing Director/Chair. They recognise you as part of the staff network and ask you how things are going in the staff network. You have about 20 seconds. What do you do? Smile sheepishly and say: *"Speak to the Chair"*? NO. So what *would* you say?

Use the space below to write down some pointers as an aide memoire.

So the mission needs to be snappy and the raison d'etre needs to be clear and concise. Ask yourself (in no particular order):

- What does a good staff network look like?
- What are our strengths, weaknesses, opportunities and threats? (SWOT analysis)
- What can you not do? (Remember, you are neither a trade union nor the HR department)
- What will you do to support the needs of the members?
- What barriers (within the network and externally) might you face?
- How can you overcome these barriers?
- How will you support each other? (both the executive team and wider membership)
- How do you ensure that you don't become a "tick box" group?
- What are the benefits to the individuals and the organisation?
- How will you sustain the life of the staff network?
- What are the risks and mitigation plan?
- How will you manage expectations?

If you are struggling to answer these questions, then it might be an idea for you to pause and spend some time finding the answers (otherwise your staff network could be prone to sickness - see *staff network maladies*). Having well-thought through answers to these questions is essential for the foundation of the staff network. The easiest (and foolish) thing would be to ignore them and hope that you will find the answers as you stumble along. Good luck with that.

You've already done this? Great; but you don't get off that easily. It may be that you've achieved some wonderful things for members in your organisation. What do you do now? How do you keep going when you have a number of successes under your belt? Take a step back and consider these questions:

1. If your staff network ceased to exist with immediate effect:

    a) Who would miss it? (note it asks who will miss the **staff network** rather than an individual)

    b) Reason for your answer.

2. What can you do about this?

The answers should help steer you towards your next steps.

Ideas on how to remain relevant:

- Periodically review your Terms of Reference (see the Game Plan).
- Survey members' experiences of the group – invite constructive criticism and suggestions.
- Invite feedback from non-members and the wider organisation.
- Get other people involved in managing the group – bring in new ideas and perspectives.

All staff networks want a foundation that will stand the test of time. If the ground is solid, staff networks will not collapse during adversity. They will, hopefully, learn to adapt, readjust and thrive.

How to start a staff network

By now, you will have done some thinking about why the staff network is needed and the types of staff networks that exist. This is the **first** important step. What do you do next? Here are an additional five practical steps you can take to help get things started.

Step 2 - Get your evidence:

- Does your organisation have a business strategy?
- What does the annual report say about diversity?
- Are there any staffing figures you can look at?
- Is there a concentration of your target group at a particular grade/range? How does this compare with similar organisations? The national picture?
- If there is a trade union representative? Could they help?
- Is there anything in the media about your target group within your employer's sector? Have an exploratory discussion with communication's team.
- Use social media tools to access information.

Step 3 - Test out the waters:

- Invite people (of all levels in the target group) to a meeting with the aim of exploring whether there is a need for a staff network.
- Set out your concerns, share the evidence gathered and have a discussion.
- Remember that just because you convened the meeting, doesn't mean that (a) people will agree with you; and (b) that you will lead the staff network.
- Who can form part of the project team (to help get things started)?

Possible discussion points for initial meetings:

- Experiences and motivations for involvement with the group.
- The current provision of support for colleagues.
- Perception of the institution in the wider community.
- In what ways a network could be of benefit and how.
- How it could operate and whom it would be open to.
- Ground rules and responsibilities.
- The group's name.

Step 4 - Learn from others:

- Speak to other staff networks in the business about their approach. Are there opportunities to collaborate on a project?
- Speak to staff networks in external organisations representing the same target group and learn from them.

Step 5 - Business case:

- Contact the corporate team that deals with the business strategy about your proposals.
- Be ready to set out the business case for the staff network.
- What resources can they provide? (e.g. facility time, budget)
- Is there someone senior that is empathetic to your aim? Champion material? (preferably someone at Board level - see chapter 8 about staff champions).

Step 6 - Build on the foundation:

- Nuts and bolts of the staff network e.g. aim, purpose, Terms of Reference, communications.

Power Tip

Just as you approach different people about how to start a staff network, the same can apply to your own support circle. Think about who you might need to engage with for advice. Areas could include:

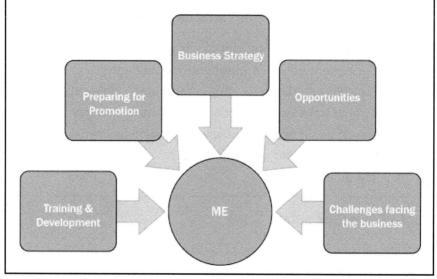

Six Steps to Starting a Staff Network

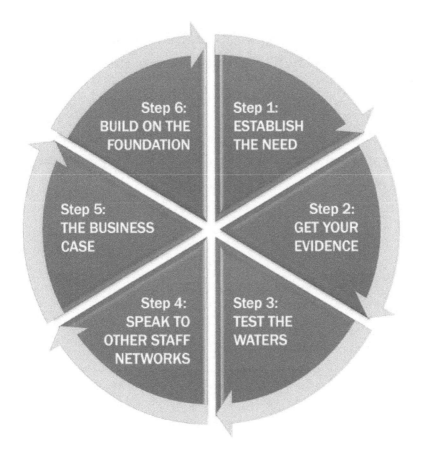

Chapter Summary

Deciding whether or not to establish (or strengthen) a staff network will require you and whoever else is involved to make a judgement call. Commonly cited benefits underline the potential of staff networks as supportive spaces for information sharing and affirmation of lived experience.

Allowing staff to air previously silenced or marginalised narratives in a safe environment, in the company of others that may have had similar or even identical work and life experiences is a good thing. It gives a sense of relief; relief that you are not alone or being over-sensitive. People need space to acknowledge the emotions, but not be a slave to them (so be solution focused).

Also, recognise that for some people in your organisation, staff networks may feel incredibly risky. What can you do or say to make the conversation safe?

A strong foundation will help to ensure the success and legacy of the staff network. In the words of Martin Luther King Jr: *"It may feel like a marathon (or even a steeplechase), but don't give up; keep building and keep moving forward."*

CHAPTER FOUR:
THE MEMBERS

"Followship, like leadership, is a role and not a destination."
(Michael McKinney)

I wanted to include a chapter about the role of the members of the staff network. An empowered, engaged and included membership is critical to the success of the staff network. However, if you want members to be active ambassadors, it is important to have an idea about who your members are and why they joined the staff network. Otherwise, how do you encourage them and offer programmes and support that they will find beneficial? Sure, you will have some general insight into what's needed but it's important that you don't assume all the answers lie with a few people (i.e. those leading the staff network).

People join staff networks for all sorts of reasons. Some join for the social engagement; for access to information; some are just curious and come for the free refreshments (let's be honest), others join out of frustration with conditions at work. Regardless of the reason, you want your members to feel that they are getting something from the staff network. You should also want them to participate, get involved and help deliver on the objectives.

For that to happen, it is important to do two things:

a) Be clear about your offer; and

b) Understand their needs and what motivates them.

I have heard many Chairs complain about the apathy of their members. They list a whole raft of activities that they have undertaken and they are at a loss as to what else they can do to 'gee' people up. They also say things like: *"You can lead a horse to water, but you can't make it drink."* If this is a scenario you can identify with, then it might be wise to take a few moments to press the pause button. Take time out to reflect, recharge and look at things objectively. Go back to basics and remind yourself what it is you are trying to do and why.

Members need to be motivated. They need to feel that the staff network is a reliable source of support and advice. But how do you motivate them? There are lots of theories on motivation - Maslow's Hierarchy of Needs, McClelland's Human Motivation Theory, Deci and Ryan's Self Determination Theory, to name a few.

But perhaps one of the best known pieces of research is that by Frederick Herzberg. Herzberg's theory of motivation showed that in general, people will be initially motivated to achieve **extrinsic** needs at work because they are unhappy without them e.g. good salary, working conditions, relationships. Once these needs are satisfied, however, the effect soon wears off - leading one to conclude that job satisfaction is only temporary. Motivation is truly realised when people satisfy the needs that Herzberg identified as **intrinsic** needs, such as achievement, advancement and personal development. These needs represent a deeper level of fulfilment.

So if we were to apply Herzberg's theory to the staff network, think about the type of things that give members the greatest satisfaction at work. What are their intrinsic needs? For example, do they want to climb the ladder? Have access to certain information? Feel valued and equal? Do they need help in holding a dfficult dialogue with their line manager? If you don't know, then ask. Do a survey, a questionnaire, lunchtime workshop, coffee mornings, whatever - but find out. Once you do, it is important to think carefully about what you will do with the results. What can you offer? What *can't* you do? Can you bring someone external into the staff network to help you? A 60-minute workshop on assertiveness training or coaching can have a greater and lasting impact than a general networking event with chocolate biscuits. Make every event and activity count; evaluation is vital.

When members believe that the staff network is actually providing for their needs (not necessarily their wants), buy-in will come. It may take time, but it will come. Members will be motivated and: *"Motivation is the energy for action"* (Edward Deci).

Calling all Members: If you are a member of a staff network, it is important for you to understand that you have a role to play in the success of the staff network. "Me?" Yes, you. You are, after all, an ambassador representing the staff network. Those leading the staff network are not responsible for the careers of members. They are there to provide information, guidance, support and to articulate the experience of members and therefore, they need your support and participation. You could be the next person to Chair the staff network, so get involved, contribute and help strengthen it.

Here are some useful things leaders of staff networks could do:

1. Remind people of the benefits of membership:

- Forum for discussion and solutions on specific issues that affect them as members.
- Knowledge sharing - increased knowledge of the organisation's agenda that can help them in their day jobs.
- Peer support - tackling problems with practical ideas.
- Communicating with management - agreeing and providing lines to take.
- Satisfaction and motivation - increases engagement.
- Career progression - access to developmental opportunities.

2. Let them know the value in:

- Attending members meetings (advertise the details of all members meetings in advance).
- Participating in network events e.g. workshops, seminars etc.
- Promoting the staff network.

3. Keep them informed about the network:

- Reinforce the mission statement.
- Remind them about the network's achievements.
- Communicate the top immediate concerns.
- Development opportunities.

Line mangers will put the work of the day as priority, which can sometimes make it difficult for members to be 'released' to attend meetings. To overcome this issue (and maximise attendance), staff networks usually organise meetings at lunchtime or whatever time suits most of the members. However, negotiating and securing time off for members to attend meetings makes a huge difference. Liaise with Human Resources to send a note to managers underlining the importance of staff networks (see sample letter in the resources section of this book).

Allowing people time to attend staff network activities

1. Demonstrates to managers and staff that networks are part of the organisation's core business.

2. Helps to legitimise and give credibility to network activities.

3. Enables more people to access meetings (not only those who have responsibility for managing their time).

4. Supports your organisation's commitment to provide developmental opportunities for staff.

Power Tip

Be prepared to invite non-members to your events. First dibs to members, and then throw it open to everyone else.

For those who cannot attend in person, are there options for people to call in using audio or video equipment? In any case, ensure that minutes and action points are clear, accurate and circulated as soon as possible after the meeting.

Celebrate the achievements of your members e.g. through email/newsletters/intranet pages. It is important to shine a light on their accomplishments because, not only does this foster a sense of togetherness, family, pride and so on, but it also helps to bust myths/preconceptions about the target group that people outside the staff network may have.

Power Advice: Suggestions to maintain member interest

- Varying content of meetings (e.g. formal alongside practical).
- Organising 'issue' based workshops and sessions.
- Inviting guest speakers.
- Encouraging members to suggest activities.
- Hosting 'get-togethers' in less formal surroundings.
- Team development activities (particularly useful when initiating a group).
- Varying the timing and location of meetings /activities.
- Not holding meetings for meetings sake.
- Sharing stories from members.

Why some people choose not to join staff networks.

As well as understanding why people join staff networks, it is necessary to be aware that just because your staff network exists and is doing great things, does not mean that all staff in the target group will want to join. As maddening as this may be, that is the reality. I have witnessed Chairs become exasperated with members of the target group who refuse to join the staff network and adopt a: *"If they're not with us, they're against us"* attitude, which is not really a healthy approach. Firstly, it is their prerogative. Joining a staff network is not compulsory. Who wants to have members who are there by force?

Secondly, some sections of the business may view membership of a staff network as *"evidence of disloyalty"* (Childs). So, if you have a member of staff who wants to progress their career, they will be keen to avoid anything that might hinder that - be it actual or perceived. According to Friedman et al, people do not join staff networks for a number of reasons including:

- There is a fear of being taunted.
- Bad reputation - staff network is riddled with in-fighting and politics and therefore they do not want to be associated/tarnished.
- Lack of interest in what is on offer.
- Don't understand how you can help them.

Rather than get annoyed, keep delivering, and keep promoting the achievements and benefits of the staff network. Leave the door open and inform them that they can be "secret supporters" or "allies" until they feel confident (this is why using the blind copy box on group emails is important). Finally, think of the many who are benefiting from your work rather than those who choose not to get involved.

Chapter Summary

It is normal for those leading staff networks to want active input and support from their membership. However, you are not responsible for the career/personal development of each member (you simply won't have the time). It is important to understand what members need and, through a variety of mechanisms, to ensure that you advocate, inform, motivate and support. You can lead a horse to water, and while you can't make it drink, you can create a thirst.

CHAPTER FIVE:
RISKS AND MALADIES

"...one thing is sure. We have to do something. We have to do the best we know how at the moment. If it doesn't turn out right, we can modify it as we go along."
(Franklin D. Roosevelt)

At the start of this book, there was a promise to tell you the truth and in that vein, it is important to be aware of the risks associated with staff networks. This chapter highlights the pitfalls, maladies and offers some remedies.

Pitfalls

1. Staff networks should provide a safe and neutral space for staff to hold discussions and find solutions to issues that matter to them. Unfortunately, many staff networks, with the best of intentions, become known as 'talking shops' because there is a lot of discussion but there are no decisions or actions. This can be construed as unproductive, self-serving, lacking respect, devoid of power and potentially divisive.

   Remedy: Publicly announce who you are, what you are doing and why you are doing it. Also, put in place a framework of action and governance as these are fundamental to the running of a successful staff network (see the Game Plan for further information). Set the agenda for members' meetings and allocate time for members to air any concerns but have a focus on seeking solutions. Facilitate effectively.

2. Staff networks are not offshoots of trade unions. Trade unions can have staff networks but not all staff networks (or their members) are

affiliated with trade unions. A trade union is a membership organisation where members pay a monthly subscription. In return, the trade union negotiates collective agreements with employers on conditions of employment including pay, disciplinary, grievance cases etc. Staff networks can have a healthy and balanced working relationship with trade unions. It is advisable that the staff network does not attempt to replicate the function of a trade union. Not only are there legal ramifications, but it could negatively impact on your relationship with the trade union representative.

Remedy: Be clear about the role of the staff network and manage the expectations of your members (failure to do so could send out the wrong messages to the organisation). Liaise with the trade union about how to get the best from the relationship and identify whether there are any areas where you can share useful intelligence to achieve mutual outcomes for your target group.

Risks

3. If a staff network is set up with little or no genuine commitment from the employer, there is a real risk of alienating staff and creating a climate of scepticism and mistrust. It won't take long for members to see through such an initiative and assume that it is merely a window-dressing exercise with little real substance. This is likely to create frustration amongst members and set back an employer's efforts to gain the trust of under-represented sections of staff.

    Remedy: Secure commitment from the organisation by carefully constructing the business case and clearly articulate what that commitment would look like for your staff network. For example, an active Board Champion, a budget/other resources, facility time, access to documents/information etc.

4. Another risk associated with setting up a staff network has to do with the possible backlash and negative reaction it could create in the wider organisation. Staff networks can be perceived by some as giving

members an 'unfair advantage'. If an employer *doesn't* take responsibility for publicising a staff network as a legitimate initiative, with the objective of redressing the historical causes of discrimination, then a staff network and its members could be subject to *unfair* criticism and resentment from within the workplace.

Remedy: Know the aim of the staff network and the reason for its existence. Using evidence to reinforce your rationale.

Power Advice (from Friedman):

An ineffective network could:

- Put back efforts to gain the trust of staff from minority groups.
- Play into the hand of cynics: *"I told you they couldn't organise themselves!"*
- Prove to doubters that there was no real need for it anyway.
- Create frustration and disillusionment amongst staff.

An effective staff network will:

- Endeavour not to become factionalised or political.
- Have a variety of activities meeting different interests.
- Be more than a social club (although social events are helpful).

Staff network maladies

It is also vital that staff networks are aware of the syndromes that can afflict them. Understanding the importance of maintaining the health of the staff network is key to unlocking the power of the staff network. Staff networks can lose their power if they neglect this aspect and as a result become susceptible to various maladies.

A common malady is 'Founders' Syndrome'. You know that one, don't you? The person who founded the staff network (or has been the Chair for a number of years) controls everything connected to it and heaven help anyone who dares to challenge their leadership style or decisions etc. Chairs that suffer with 'Founders' Syndrome' believe that they are the authority on issues relating to their target group; no one could be more passionate than they are; who could possibly run the staff network better than they? Do you know who founded the staff network? They did. They were there from the beginning.

(Please note that I am not assuming that all long-standing Chairs of staff networks suffer with 'Founders' Syndrome'.)

Unfortunately, this is not the only syndrome that attacks staff networks. See the following table for some others.

Common staff network maladies

Diagnosis	Symptoms	Possible Cure	Caution/Risk
Founders' Syndrome - this condition can be quite toxic for staff networks. Mainly affecting Chairs/leaders, they see the staff network as part and parcel of their identity. It's a way of showcasing their success. They like the power it brings and feel threatened by anyone who has a different vision for the staff network. Can sometimes be divisive in their conduct - all for the sake of the staff network (apparently).	1. Has been the Chair/lead of the staff network for a considerable length of time (three years and more). 2. They see the staff network as 'theirs' / 'their baby' 3. Can be quite authoritarian in their leadership style. 4. Adverse to suggestions to change / improving the staff network (they take it as a personal attack). 5. Use every opportunity to remind people that they started the staff network / or were there from the early days.	• Succession planning strategy needs to be revisited or instigated. • Time to pass on the baton. Is there a senior member that can broker this discussion in a safe environment?	**HIGH RISK:** May adopt a resistant or defensive attitude. Remember that the Chair aligns their success/identity to the staff network and therefore will need to find an alternative role that will help tap into their knowledge and experience.

71

Diagnosis	Symptoms	Possible Cure	Caution/Risk
Myopia (short-sightedness) - where the staff networks fails to plan strategically and appear to be constantly focused on NOW.	1. No strategy in place 2. Reluctant to discuss the future. 3. Appears confused.	• Vision test essential - need to think how the staff network impacts on members and the organisation. • Revisit the aim of the staff network and put in place an action plan. • Liaise with other staff networks for inspiration and advice.	Low Risk
Event-itis - connects success of the staff network with the number of events they can organise and attendees.	1. Organises event after event but there is no evidence of learning due to lack of evaluation. 2. A good event means that the staff network must be doing well. 3. More interested in output rather than outcome. 4. Prefer to have drinks rather than focus on development.	• EVALUATION. Look at the *outcome* of the events, not just numbers in attendance. Five elements to a successful event **S.P.I.D.E.R.** *(Strategically Plan, Implement, Deliver, EVALUATE, Review)* What are people learning from the events? If your budget was cut, what would you do? • Review of what it is the network is trying to achieve.	**CAUTION:** People who are effective at organising successful events may be offended. Assure them that their skills are valuable. Explain that the execution is not in question but rather the outcome.

Diagnosis	Symptoms	Possible Cure	Caution/Risk
The 'talk talk' network - promises an ocean, delivers a puddle	**Values:** 1. Style over substance. 2. Rhetoric over reality. 3. Debate overdelivery.	• Consider the reputation of the staff network. • Get back to the reason why you started. Why aren't you delivering? If you lack skills in the team, recruit. • Set out a plan of action and ***under promise, over deliver***	Low risk
The Glory Seeker - enjoys and relishes the kudos and the position of Chair but rarely delivers anything. When challenged, takes on a victim mentality. 'Gate-keeps' information.	1. On a permanent power trip. 2. Loves the position but shuns the responsibility. 3. Verbose, vain and plays the victim when they don't get their own way. 4. Content to ride on the success of others and claim them as their own but offers no reciprocity.	Needs to be made aware of their behaviour. Gather evidence. Options: 1. You can subtly call attention to the behaviour; 2. Directly confront them (with grace) in a safe environment outlining the impact of their behaviour; 3. Approach a critical friend to act as mediator to help to broker a way forward.	**HIGH RISK:** May have a similar reaction to someone suffering from Founders' Syndrome - which may lead to conflict. See chapter 7 on managing conflict.

Do any of these sound familiar? These are just *some* of the maladies that can cause a crack in the foundation of a staff network. If you ignore the cracks, however small, the staff network will start to crumble and eventually collapse - causing serious damage. So take your staff network for regular check-ups.

Chapter Summary

There are a number of pitfalls that staff networks need to be mindful of. Taking the time to reflect on the risks and remedies in this section within the context of your organisation requires courage, determination, objectivity and empathy.

The staff network is a vehicle for change. As you steer it in the right direction, stay on course and remember to:

- Embrace change and hold to your values.
- Build confidence and self-esteem.
- Point to a positive future.
- Lead with your heart as well as your head.

Take the staff network for a regular MOT.

CHAPTER SIX:
THE GAME PLAN

"Teamwork makes the dream work."
(John C. Maxwell)

If you've made it to this section, it must be assumed that you have tackled the 'what' and 'why' of your staff network – which is excellent as it makes the game plan much easier to execute.

The game plan, or Terms of Reference (ToR) or Constitution, is the document or framework that describes the specifics of the strategy of the staff network. It is much more than a mere set of guidelines within which the staff network can function. It is the blueprint which the staff network refers to in order to ensure it carries out its duties for the purpose that it was established. However, time and time again, ToRs are written in a haphazard way at the genesis of the staff network and are rarely revisited unless there is conflict within the management team/executive committee.

In writing the game plan, it is important for leaders of staff networks to understand three things:

1. That this is a plan of action designed to achieve a long-term overall aim;

2. That the TOR is for the members to hold the executive team to account as well as to protect the staff network;

3. That they should think beyond their tenure (legacy mentality).

> **Power Observation:** Staff network leaders suffering with *'Founder' Syndrome'* may find the last one in particular difficult to grasp!

There are many different styles of ToR – some are very complicated while others are so simple to the extent that they are open to misinterpretation. The key is to cover the main elements as clearly as possible so that members, stakeholders and successors can pick these up and run with them. It is vital for the ToR to be open and C.R.Y.S.T.A.L™ clear.

C	Challenging and Collaborative - What is it you want to change and who will you work with to get this done?
R	Resourceful - Finances may be limited so how will you operate within a stringent environment? What resources do you already have at your disposal?
Y	Yearning for improvement - Describe how the target group and organisation will improve as a result of the staff network's input.
S	Strengthen the members - Are you looking out for the interests of your members? How do you know this? Evidence? How do you intend to build resilience and empower members of your staff network?
T	Transparent - Is it clear what the staff network is doing? The impact being made? Are you a trusted source of information?
A	Accountable - Who is the staff network accountable to? Who are your critical friends?
L	Lead the way - How will you make a difference for your members and ultimately improve the corporate health of the business? Shine a light on what needs to be improved, how the staff network can provide solutions and shout about your results.

All good ToRs should cover the following:

Time (the when):

- Running a staff network takes passion, vision, commitment and time. Ensure you secure facility time for at least the Chair, but preferably for everyone on the executive/core/management team. It is important to point out that you may have to 'earn' your facility time. Why should you be given additional time to discuss issues that only affect a minority? Adopt a cost benefit analysis mindset and think about the organisation's return on investment.

Background (the what):

- A brief description of the background to the staff network and why it exists.

  For example: *The Green Eyed Managers' staff network exists to:*

  i) Provide GEMS with a voice through empowerment and support;

  ii) Represent the interests of GEMS within the organisation; and

  iii) Work with senior management to build an organisation where equity and equality of opportunities exists for all.

Vision and mission statement (the why):

- A compelling vision statement can inspire others to get involved. It expresses the aspiration and intention of a staff network. It should be brief and easy to understand and communicate.
- A mission statement is the 'what and why'. It is more action oriented. It should be concise and clarify the network's overall purpose.

Goals/Workplan (the how):

"Goals are dreams with deadlines" (Napoleon Hill, American author)

- This should be an action plan with deliverables and timelines. The plan which outlines to members and other parties the work undertaken by the core team. Not only does this inform people of what you are trying to achieve, but also widens their understanding of the scale. Please, please, please remember the Golden Rule:

UNDER PROMISE, OVER DELIVER

- Do not commit to tasks that your staff network cannot deliver (remember the 'talk talk' malady). Suggestions for headings on the action plan could include:
  - Key Goals
  - Tasks
  - Deliverables
  - Dates/Timescales
  - Owners
  - Status (achieved, ongoing etc)
  - Comments

- You may also want to consider doing an annual summary or report informing members and stakeholders of your work throughout the year. You could also offer this as a developmental opportunity to members. Keep meticulous records of your output (intended aims) and highlight the outcomes (actual impact). Your achievements are your arsenal in times of uncertainty.

Scope:

- What is the responsibility and authority of the staff network?
- What does it need to address and what is outside its area of concern?

Membership:

- Is there a criteria for membership?
- Are there any restrictions? Why?
- What is the process for selecting members on the committee?
- How do people join?
- What is the role of members? (members have a responsibility too)
- Can groups as well as individuals join?
- Are there different levels of membership?
- How can members raise concerns or seek redress?

Inclusive versus Exclusive Membership - There are benefits of being exclusive (staff network members only), and inclusive (opening up to wider membership).

Exclusive	Inclusive
Provides a dedicated space to support an under-represented group.	Might hinder the potential of a network to become a supportive space to disclose and share sensitive information.
Could be perceived within the organisation as insular and reinforce divisions.	Could increase understanding and recognition of discrimination within an organisation.
Encourages people who may not feel comfortable with aspects of their identity (i.e. not out, hidden impairment) to participate.	Some people might feel put off and disinclined to participate for fear of revealing too much about themselves.
Experiences and issues could remain 'in' the group, without the means to do anything about them.	People with an interest in or specialist knowledge could make valuable contributions in supporting the work of the group.

Some staff networks have a membership list (for target group members only) and an allies list (for supporters of the staff network).

Resources and budget:

- What resources does the group have at its disposal (space, funding, staffing, time etc.)?
- Is there a budget? If yes, what are you going to spend it on? (food/ beverages should not be your only answer.) If you don't have a budget, what are your options?
- What other 'currency' do you have?

Governance or decision-making:

- How will the group be organised?
- What are the different roles and responsibilities (e.g. Chair, Vice-Chair, communications officer etc.)?
- Will there be committees/sub-groups/workstreams? If so, what are their roles and responsibilities?
- How will decisions be made (voting, consensus, etc.)?
- Is there a requirement for a certain number of people (quorum) to be present to pass a decision/motion?
- How will you handle inefficiency?
- How will you handle any conflict?

Meetings:

- How often will the executive/management team meet?
- How often will you meet with members? When and where?

Reviewing terms of reference:

- Timeframe for review? By whom and how?

Network Champion:

- Do you need a senior person to champion your staff network? (yes, you do - see the section on staff champions under chapter 8)

Critical Friends:

- Consider having a group of critical friends - those who know enough about the organisation can provide critical yet insightful and practical advice. Be clear about their role, expectation, time involved etc.

Communication:

- How will you communicate with your members? Bulletin-type email? Newsletter?
- How will you communicate with external partners? (Important to consider, as they may not be interested in a lot of the internal information that your members need).

- Consider sending emails using the 'blind copy' option. It protects the membership and those who wish to support the network anonymously.
- If you plan to use social media to promote the staff network, it is wise to consider devising a social media marketing strategy. Your brand is very important, so getting the basics right from the outset is vital. Liaise with the communications team (if there is one) to explore and identify how best to protect the organisation's brand and ensure the messages dovetail.

Power Tip: Using Social Media

Social media is a powerful way to share information and interact with your members and wider audience.

- Think carefully about the social media tools you choose and how you plan to use them for maximum effect.
- Find your audience.
- Spend time to get the basics right and be clear about your mission. Creating a strong social media profile is a valuable online business card that can, when done correctly, impress your audience. You only have one opportunity to create the right first impression.
- Build a relationship with your target audience by sharing valuable content.
- Remember to protect the employer brand.

PLEASE BE AWARE: *Your organisation may have certain protocols regarding how staff networks use social media to engage with the public, so please seek advice from the relevant communications team.*

Ideas on how to remain relevant:

- Periodically review your terms of reference.
- Survey members' experiences of the group – invite constructive criticism and suggestions.
- Invite feedback from non-members and the wider organisation.
- Get other people involved in managing the group – bring in new ideas and perspectives.

If you're involved in setting up a new staff network and you tackle these issues head-on, then it should make life so much easier. You will feel focused, energised and confident. If the legacy of the staff network is at the forefront of your mind, the ToR will reflect this.

However, if like some, you joined the leadership of an established staff network that neglected to put these things in place or maybe had a different priority, be prepared to face some resistance. Why? Some people resist introducing or amending ToR for a variety of reasons:

i)   They lack a real understanding of what they are.

ii) They're comfortable with the lack of formal terms as they prefer to avoid being held accountable for their decisions and deliverables (or lack thereof) during their 'term in office' (which leads one to ask the question, why get involved at such a senior level in the first place?).

iii) They are threatened by change and what this could mean for their 'position'.

Power Advice

People who resist change aren't against you personally.

Look beyond the emotion, broaden your shoulders and think of the bigger picture. Remind them that a strong ToR is important for the foundation of the network and subsequently, the legacy of the staff network.

Code of conduct

Why include something about a code of conduct? I have learnt that when emotions run high, some people may behave in ways that surprise them on later reflection. So it's important to lay down values and principles of behaviour that help to foster a positive environment.

It is also fundamental that the Chair and the management team/executive committee agree some sort of Code of Conduct about how they will work with each other both behind closed doors and in public. It is important for staff network teams to agree that they should not act in a way that risks harm to the reputation of:

    a. themselves;
    b. the staff network;
    c. the organisation;
    d. the sector; and
    e. the representative community.

Managing internal conflict

Conflict is often healthy and can be useful in uncovering a wealth of unmet needs. Staff networks are not required to agree all the time. They are, however, required to resolve and manage conflict constructively.

Challenges and disagreements are bound to happen, but the handling can either destroy or deepen a relationship. I know that staff networks can get snared and bogged down with personality clashes, feelings of insecurities, and personal agenda. Having to deal with this is an additional burden that sucks out the energy required to tackle the bigger issues that the staff network was set up to deal with in the first place. From time to time, the network may experience internal problems or disputes about how it is being run, what is being achieved, balance of roles and work within the team etc. That's normal. However, how you handle this is so important. The staff network is not a launderette, so don't air your dirty washing for all to see and hear. When a staff network does this, the impact is devastating - especially if you've worked hard to build the reputation of the staff network. It stays in the minds of people and they may begin to disassociate themselves from the staff network. Therefore, it is vital that you learn how to resolve conflict in a safe way which is generally not played out like a scene from a Greek tragedy on the main stage.

If you have tried to resolve things amongst yourselves but to no avail, please seek mediation. Mediation provides an opportunity to speak directly with each other in an informal, productive atmosphere to develop a mutually satisfying resolution. There are numerous benefits of managing internal conflict. These include:

- Helping to prevent further conflict .
- Resolving disputes/issues quickly.
- Reconciling differences.
- Regaining momentum.
- Improving communication.
- Preventing misunderstanding.
- Building relationships based on mutual trust.
- Providing greater harmony in the staff network.
- Increasing longevity and productivity of the management team.

Remember - the staff network comes first. If you need to bring in an external person, make sure this is someone that can be objective, trusted, is discreet and believes in the staff network e.g. a critical friend/ally.

Chapter Summary

The game plan is largely based on trust. It will only work when everyone responsible for leading the staff network agrees to honour each other and abide by the Terms of Reference. By all means, tweak the plan, but don't sabotage the game.

Plan the work. Work the plan. Be victorious.

CHAPTER SEVEN:
THE TEAM

"Coming together is a beginning. Keeping together is progress. Working together is success."
(Henry Ford)

This chapter aims to help you understand some key factors to be aware of when forming a leadership team to run the staff network. There is no such thing as the perfect team but there are some things that you can put in place to help ensure that the team works in a harmonious way.

Leading with Grace

Being in a position of leadership is like being at the helm of a ship – smooth sailing at times, having to handle squalls at others. But like the captain, you must know where you're heading (big picture) and plot the course accordingly so that the crew and passengers are aware of what to expect as part of the journey.

Leading a staff network requires you to bring this skill of straddling big picture stuff and the detail that brings both texture and depth to relationships. It is a learned skill rather than some kind of exclusive innate quality that inhabits the realms of a super-elite. Wendy Irwin, writer and expert on diversity, calls this skill graceful leadership. Before you imagine staff networks donning tutus, ballet shoes and pirouetting through the corridors of your workplace, below she explains what she means.

Leading with grace is essentially about the staff network understanding how to deliver their goals and objectives through people in ways that promote their dignity and that of others. It is about generating a sense of purpose and care in that quest; whatever the staff network, regardless of the industry, irrespective of the circumstances.

This is not a skill that should be operated by the staff network Chair alone, but a skill and understanding that every member of the network needs to comprehend and demonstrate. The benefits generated will be useful to them individually and as a purposive collective.

Defining grace

Grace in one form or another has been part of our lexicon for centuries. Grace is derived from the Latin *gratus* which means pleasing or thankful to what many see as a contemporary proxy, respect. Groups and individuals recognise this. The term **grace** absolutely has its foundations in a particular belief system but that doesn't mean that it isn't useful to the contemporary work context. Other ways of defining grace highlight its action-orientation as well as its ability to build, maintain and possibly recover mutually-advantageous relationships that balance honesty and respect as well as reciprocity and common purpose.

- *Noun* Smoothness and elegance of movement
- *Noun* Courteous good will
- *Verb* To bring honour or credit to (someone or something) by one's attendance and participation.

So what does this have to do with being part of a staff network or even leading one? The answer is that it has an awful lot to do with this work. Grace is a dynamic and context-specific set of behaviours that involve perspective-taking (even when you don't want to do it), creating the conditions for trust (even when your own trust conditions have been damaged) and generosity (when those around you behave in miserly ways).

Many years ago, I had the pleasure of meeting a group of graduates who were on the NHS graduate training scheme. Bright-eyed and brimming with energy and enthusiasm, I spoke to them at length about what their training and development had highlighted to them about themselves.

Their answers were surprising in many ways. Firstly, nearly all of them spoke at length about the technical training that they had received, from time management, project management to the more classical management and leadership training. What was surprising was the wisdom that some of them spoke with about the lessons learned about themselves. They spoke about integrity, relationship-building and curiously, empathy.

Without doubt, their ability to master the technical skills from finance to people management were fundamental to their success in the NHS. Yet the added value of building and developing skills that helped deliver outcomes in a way that built reciprocity, trust and engagement seemed to make potentially abrasive transactions smoother. The ability and willingness to understand or even be curious about the wants and needs of other parties is essential to developing these personal resources. With those graduates who understood the added value of graciousness in their work lives, there was the understanding that there were many ways to arrive at a good decision as well as many ways to implement it effectively. One of the cornerstones to this was thinking empathetically.

Building empathy is not the same as sympathy, they aren't even close companions. Empathy is defined. The ability to be curious about a perspective that isn't yours is an intellectual skill that we often forget to exercise or pay enough attention to in order to nurture it properly.

Grace and empathy are two critical assets that successful staff networks need to develop a trade in if they are to survive in organisations that may (because of financial constraints) begin to ask questions about the role and purpose of staff networks.

Corporate empathy

Staff networks can be particularly successful when they build an organisational corporate empathy, an understanding of what is it like to experience a particular process or product from a perspective that does naturally belong to them (remember the quote from Harper Lee mentioned in the second chapter?).

The ability to take a perspective that does not naturally come to you is a powerful cognitive skill that should be nurtured. Part of utilising the power of staff networks can be their ability to lead the organisations that they work within to a position of cognitive empathy.

It is critical then, that the staff networks think carefully about how this grace plays out in terms of their day-to-day experience:

- Are staff network members gracious to each other, even when they disagree about the most fundamental things?
- Is the staff network gracious to its host organisation, moving in a way that is elegant and smooth in terms of navigating difficult, sometimes circumspect and treacherous organisational processes?
- Does the staff network pace and lead the business into forms of empathic thinking so that better quality decisions are made on behalf of clients and customers as well as those members of staff?

Ways to achieve this

You can model graciousness as a particular behavioural skill that you choose to demonstrate. What would someone see that was different?

1. An ability to see past an initial problem to a particular opportunity to get results and build, maintain and restore relationships.

2. Self-awareness. Leading with grace isn't always about being beatific and saintly. It involves a genuine and honest assessment of your own skills and abilities to be gracious when the temptation might be to respond to being hurt and disrespected by causing hurt, confusion and adding to the swamp of disrespect.

3. Have a contract with yourself. As the staff network lead, you need to activate your grace stocks by recognising that you are the ambassador of your staff network brand. Unfairly but realistically, many will judge you and your reactions to difficult circumstances as being typical and representative of everybody who identifies as being part of your staff network.

4. Start to think of yourself and the staff network as being part of a business within a business. It doesn't matter if your organisation is part of the public sector, a social enterprise, a charity or a private sector organisation. Every staff network needs an entrepreneurial streak that focuses on adding value to the business and building their empathy capital as a minimum.

Generosity

Generosity is a key ingredient to leading with grace. It is quite a significant request to encourage us to think about generosity when money and other resources are scarce. Generosity, according to the Oxford Dictionary, means: *"Showing a readiness to give more of something than is expected"* and this can be delivered in creative ways. For example, as the staff network lead, you may have to take risks and engage in those costly crucial conversations. Few may understand the work that you have to do both overtly and covertly, fewer still may have the grace to acknowledge you for it.

A key component in leading a staff network is how we relate with others in the workplace. Leading with empathy and generosity will help to create our reputation and determine whether our interactions and transactions are abrasive or graceful.

Excerpts from *'Space for Grace'* © by Wendy Irwin

Building the leadership team

In the 1980s, there was a fantastic American TV programme called **THE A-TEAM**. It was about a fictional group of ex-United States Army Special Forces personnel who worked as soldiers of fortune while on the run from the Army for a crime they didn't commit. The A-Team were the good guys who helped the oppressed. In each episode, members of the A-Team would find themselves in a quandary or trapped and needing to do something to overcome the 'baddies'. It didn't matter whether they were locked in a fireworks warehouse, a prison cell or an abandoned building, the A-Team would devise a plan based on the skill of the team, and the resources at hand. The upshot was they always overcame the baddies and at the end, Colonel John 'Hannibal' Smith would say, *"I love it when a plan comes together"*.

Not every staff network leader has the luxury of choosing their 'A-Team' but like this fictional group, it is a case of having a plan, working with who you have and doing the best with what you've got. That means understanding the resources at your disposal, the skills of the team and belief in the plan (it also means recognising what skills are absent). For that to happen effectively, it is important to create the right environment to enable the management team (committee/executive) to perform at their best while at the same time enabling them to have a degree of autonomy in their work. It also means that the management team should be prepared to do their 'homework' about the position they are in.

Staff networks should provide the notable opportunity for continuing professional development, not least for the members on the management team. The additional responsibility within the staff network should allow members to develop a range of skills and competencies that may not be afforded to them in their day-to-day roles.

Benefits for individuals include:

- Peer support.
- Networking opportunities.
- Access to information on issues affecting them.
- Feeling that their opinion helps to make a difference.
- Targeted training sessions.
- Coaching and mentoring.
- Discussion forums.
- Opportunities to develop skills and competencies.

Have an objective about your role in the staff network as part of your performance appraisal process. Also, everyone in the management team should consider undertaking some sort of skills audit/workstyle analysis. Not only will this tap into people's strengths but it will also identify areas of development that will help in the wider organisation. Meredith Belbin's work on team roles is often used to investigate how individuals behave or what functions they perform in a group. **Belbin identifies nine group roles, or clusters of behaviour. These roles have been categorised as either function (or task)** - oriented or cerebral (people-oriented), fitting with the task and relationship roles of leadership. Belbin's team roles are:

Team Role	Contribution	Allowable Weakness
Plant	Creative, imaginative, free-thinking. generates ideas and solves difficult problems.	Ignores incidentals. Too preoccupied to communicate effectively.
Resource Investigator	Outgoing, enthusiastic, communicative. Explores opportunities and develops contacts.	Over-optimistic. Loses interest once initial enthusiasm has passed.
Coordinator/ Chair	Mature, confident, identifies talent. Clarifies goals. Delegates effectively.	Can be seen as manipulative. Offloads own share of the work.
Shaper	Challenging, dynamic, thrives on pressure. Has the drive and courage to overcome obstacles.	Prone to provocation. Offends people's feelings.
Monitor Evaluator	Sober, strategic and discerning. Sees all options and judges accurately.	Lacks drive and ability to inspire others. Can be overly critical.

Teamworker	Cooperative, perceptive and diplomatic. Listens and averts friction.	Indecisive in crunch situations. Avoids confrontation.
Implementer	Practical, reliable, efficient. Turns ideas into actions and organises work that needs to be done.	Somewhat inflexible. Slow to respond to new possibilities.
Complete Finisher	Painstaking, conscientious, anxious. Searches out errors. Polishes and perfects.	Inclined to worry unduly. Reluctant to delegate.
Specialist	Single-minded, self starting, dedicated. Provides knowledge and skills in rare supply.	Contributes only on a narrow front. Dwells on technicalities.

Roles and descriptions courtesy of Belbin Associates

Do you recognise yourself (or anyone else) in these descriptions? It is important to get a balance of these types to be an effective team. Finding a way to understand the skills and strengths of those around the management team table will make a great difference when divvying up roles and tasks. See the management team as a safe group for growth and development. What can you learn from others and what can they learn from you?

Power Wisdom

You may not be the Chair of the staff network but remember every Chair needs an excellent Deputy (Number Three, Number Four etc). Find your place and do your best to support the staff network. Use your time on the core team to hone a range of skills and competencies. Remember, competence yields confidence.

Getting the best from your management team meetings

One of the biggest causes of tension in staff network management teams is when people fail to do what they signed up to do.

Have you ever encountered the following scenario?

At the end of the meeting, the person leading it sums up what's been agreed and what's going to happen. Everyone nods. At the next meeting, the person leading it asks people to say what they've done. People look at their feet and mutter: "*Sorry, I haven't done it; I was too busy.*"

Has this ever happened to you when leading either a team meeting or a one-to-one meeting? Larry Reynolds (21st Century Leader©) offers suggestions on what you can do to prevent it happening next time.

- When it comes to agreeing action, don't summarise what you expect the other person to do and wait for them to nod. Instead, ask them: "*What will you do as a result of this meeting?*" If the other person says it, it makes it much more likely they will actually do it.
- Push for specifics. If they say: "*I'll write a paper for the next meeting*", ask them: "*By when? Who will you send it to? Roughly how long will the document be?*" The more specific a commitment, the more likely it will be carried out.
- Probe their commitment. If your hunch is that the person is less than wholeheartedly committed to doing whatever it is, probe a bit. You might say: "*Can I just check that you are really able to do this?*" Or: "*On a 0-10 scale, how certain are you that you can*

deliver this?" If the number is low, ask what would make it higher. Obviously how you phrase the question depends on the context and your relationship with that person, but if your sense is that they are not really committed, don't just leave it and hope for the best. Probe a little bit more and find out what might increase their commitment.

There's a tough balance between meeting the demands of the day job and those of the staff network. The allocated time you have for staff network business is limited and therefore, it is vital that it is used efficiently and effectively.

Squad X (the fifth wheel)

"Criticism, like rain, should be gentle enough to nourish a man's growth without destroying his roots." (Frank A Clarke)

Squad X refers to that person or group of people who have the wrong mindset for a successful staff network. They constantly criticise the staff network. But unlike rain that nourishes the staff network, Squad X is like a weed. The new shorter Oxford English Dictionary describes a weed as *"...a plant not valued for use or beauty, growing wild and rank, and regarded as cumbering the ground or hindering the growth of superior vegetation... unprofitable, troublesome, or noxious growth."*

That aptly describes Squad X. They sit alongside the staff network sucking all the energy with their criticism, hindering the growth of the staff network with their negativity, and are troublesome and noxious.

They always want to be at the heart of the staff network but don't have the staff network in their heart. It is important for anyone who has a desire to run a successful staff network to be aware of Squad X. They pick holes in 90% of everything the staff network does. They perceive themselves as the fifth column - sabotaging the staff network from within for the greater good of the members, when in reality, they are the fifth wheel - of absolutely no use to anyone.

Some of their characteristics include:

- Their comments/input are destructive rather than constructive.
- They are reactionary rather than proactive.
- Their suggestions lack thought and substance (but when not taken up, claim that they are being ignored/squeezed out).
- They want control but offer no reciprocity.
- Deep down, they want to lead the staff network but lack the wherewithal (and they know this - hence the attitude). They therefore complain and say things like: *"Well, when so-and-so was the Chair, we never did that."* (even though they probably criticised the Chair at that time too.)
- They come together with the sole purpose of trying to undermine the work of the staff network but they have no loyalty to each other at all.
- They use the arena of the staff network meeting to settle personal scores.
- They openly (publicly) criticise the staff network and say things like: *"I don't want to be part of the problem; I want to be part of the solution. So I will hang on in there and try to help turn things around."*
- They lack self-awareness and integrity.
- They have their own self-interest uppermost in their mind.
- They want to be involved but they rarely actively contribute and usually absolve themselves from any responsibility to deliver.
- Squad X is very demanding without offering any assistance. They also expect others will manage around them. They'll turn up at an event, for example, and ask: *"What is my role here?"* (*and shamelessly take equal credit*).

Whether it is intentional or not, the purpose of Squad X is to undermine - be it the staff network leadership or the work of the staff network itself.

Here are two suggestions for handling Squad X:

- Keep achieving and ensure that your achievements are visible. Recruit and empower ambassadors to highlight your achievements too (that's the best weedkiller!). Do not get drawn into petty arguments with them as that will zap your energy and leave you feeling despondent, weary and ready to throw in the towel.

- Be positive and challenge them to solve their own problems, e.g. *"You make a valid point. How do YOU suggest we resolve it?"* (then look out for the tumbleweed.)

Not all criticism is bad, of course. But the Squad X type of criticism is, as Celestine Chua (Personal Excellence) describes: *"...an uncanny ability to scrutinise and zoom into every little problem there is. Following which, they fixate on these issues and offer unwanted opinions on them."*

If you try really, really, hard, you can find a positive thing about Squad X - they can keep you focused and sharp. In all your key decisions, you will consider: *"What are they going to say?"* and you prepare your 'lines to take' so that the team are all singing from the same hymn sheet. A unified response is a powerful one.

Criticism is to be expected, not just from Squad X but from anyone who either doesn't understand, doesn't like or feels threatened by your staff network.

Power Advice

Squad X might not be aware that they demonstrating a negative or unhelpful mentality. They may have legitimate concerns or suggestions. Therefore, whether or not you believe that they have something constructive to say, listen attentively just in case they are trying to offer an opinion that's misinterpreted due to their lack of tact.

Power tips for handling critical people:

- **Do not take it personally** - The criticisms reflect more about who they are rather than who you are. They may have certain beliefs and frameworks about life.
- **Be objective** (Seek the hidden message) - Put aside the delivery and focus on the content of what is being said.

- **Act responsibly** - Just because they are dishing out the criticism does not mean you have to react in anger. Since the person must have a lot of angst to be voluntarily dispensing criticisms in the first place, your retaliation will probably only invite more of such comments. This debate is one which is unlikely to end well.

- **Reject it** - Just as the critical people need to take responsibility for their comments, recipients have to take responsibility for receiving the negativity too. With every occurrence, there is always the event itself, and the perception of the event. You can't change how people want to act or what they say, but you can change how you act around them. There is always a choice. The negativity is not yours if you don't take it.

- **Communicate** the features and benefits of the staff network - reinforcing the outcomes can help dispel assumptions.

- **Show them kindness** - WHAT? You are probably wondering: "*Why should I be kind to them? They most certainly don't deserve kindness.*" That, my friend, is grace.

Chapter Summary

The team is the driving force behind the staff network. It is essential that each team member knows their role in the team, understands how best they can contribute, respects and encourages each other (grace and generosity), and believes in the mission. Those are the golden rules of **THE A-TEAM**.

CHAPTER EIGHT:
ALIGNING THE STAFF NETWORK WITH THE BUSINESS

"The most important single ingredient in the formula of success is knowing how to get along with people."
(Theodore Roosevelt)

This chapter looks at the benefits of a firm and fruitful relationship with senior management. It also highlights the importance and paybacks of a staff network Champion. Whether you work for the private sector, public sector or the civil society sector, your organisation is engaged in some sort of business, in some sort of marketplace.

Relationship with senior management

The relationship between staff networks and 'the management' is a delicate one. Employers aren't against staff networks *per se*. Not really. What some managers may be against is something which takes staff away from their day job to attend a meeting that apparently has nothing to do with their day job; they cannot see the value. They could be averse to something because they don't have a proper grasp of it.

From the earliest days of network groups, some senior managers (those with less personal experience with staff networks) have approached them fearing that they might become unions or clusters of angry people. They also have expressed anxiety about their power and the kinds of complaints or demands they may express (Friedman et al). Research by Bert Klandermans (Professor of Applied Psychology, Amsterdam University) showed that staff networks are perceived to be driven primarily by a dynamic of frustration and aggression and therefore staff networks are divisive.

How do you change this perception? How do staff networks help managers to understand that just because a group of employees are dissatisfied does not mean it will lead to antagonism? Tough question.

Let's look at this from another angle. At the heart of a relationship between the employee and the employer is trust. What do I mean by trust?

"Trust is a primary factor in how people work together, listen to one another, and build effective relationships. Yet many people are unaware of the actions that influence trust. Trust is a critical link to all good relationships, both personal and professional."

(Ken Blanchard, management expert)

The Chartered Institute of Personnel and Development (CIPD) state that trust is fundamental to sustained and effective relationships. They identified four elements of trust that employees expect to see:

- Ability – demonstrable competence at doing their job;
- Benevolence – a concern for others beyond their own needs and having benign motives;
- Integrity – adherence to a set of principles acceptable to others encompassing fairness and honesty; and
- Predictability – a regularity of behaviour over time.

Blanchard also says that:

"Lack of trust creates cynicism, doubt, and anxiety that leads to 'time off-task' speculation and generally low energy and low productivity. When people don't trust their leaders, they don't come toward something; they pull back and withdraw instead. They doubt rather than cooperate."

Power Fact

CIPD figures show that trust is particularly weak in the public sector. Public sector workers are much less likely to profess trust in their senior leaders than those in the private sector (despite private sector trust crises in banking, retail, energy etc.).

If staff networks can demonstrate that they can help build trust between the employer and employees (through how they operate) and provide a collective voice, perhaps they can be seen as a key player in employee engagement; engaged and committed employees lead to increased productivity.

An independent inquiry into the world of work by Ed Sweeney (Making Work Better: an agenda for government) says: *"Studies by ACAS and others show that employees want some form of "voice" at work and more cooperative styles of engagement with management. As the labour market experts at Warwick University's business school observe: 'This search for "voice" is not just to meet the needs of employees, important though that is. We know that the experience of involvement is closely associated with positive employee evaluations of management responsiveness.' (Bryson, Charlwood and Forth). This feeds through into productivity. The more extensive the range of voice systems used in organisations, the more likely it was that managers reported benefits from increased output to declining absenteeism (Sisson). Voice systems which combine "embedded" direct forms of involvement with indirect voice via representative bodies are strongly associated with higher levels of organisational commitment (Purcell and Georgiades)."*

To start building or strengthening the relationship with senior managers, you may need to do some digging to find answers to questions such as:

- Are you aware of what is happening in the organisation?
- Do you know the workplace culture?
- What are the issues facing the business?
- What is working well?

- What is at the top of your CEOs in-tray?
- What was discussed at the last board meeting?
- What are the priorities of the HR Director?

Why do you need to do this?

You want to demonstrate that your staff network is concerned with the overall health of the organisation and, while you cannot fix all the problems, you might be able to offer solutions to some of them based on the valuable information gleaned from members in your staff network. It conveys wide canvas thinking. It highlights a sensitivity to the issues faced by the upper echelons of the business. It demonstrates your unique ability to act as a conduit. It shines a light on your people power and resourcefulness. Sonia Brown (National Black Women's Network) concurs with this approach:

"Staff networks should not work in silos but need to keep abreast of what's happening in the wider organisation."

Case Study: Ability UK Employee Resource Group (HSBC Bank)

HSBC believes that having a diverse workforce brings great value and strength to the business. The international bank has more than 50 Employee Resource Groups (ERGs) with 15,000 members globally who help foster an inclusive working environment. Ability Network UK (Ability) is the HSBC ERG for disability and carers. It is a key strategic partner in engaging and supporting employees who experience disability in the UK. Ability has developed a clear strategy closely aligned with HSBC values of being dependable, open and connected. Ability delivers:

- Peer-to-peer support by creating connections and leveraging the knowledge of colleagues with shared experience.
- Signposting to internal resources (e.g. HR, OH, counselling etc.) and to external resources (e.g. charities and professionals).

- Member events – raising the profile of disability in the workplace, both generally and with topic specific information.

Ability acts as a valuable point of connection between HSBC and employees with lived experience of disability. Members share insight on the provision of accessible services for customers, for example the accessibility of online and mobile banking.

Ability also offers important support for leaders and line managers of employees with a disability. Gary Denton, Chairperson of Ability UK, explains: *"Inevitably line managers will manage people with health conditions and disabilities that they have no experience of. It's understandable that managers may sometimes find this challenging, so we are happy to help them fit the various pieces like HR, OH, assessments, workplace adjustments and personal support into one complete picture."*

One of Ability's achievements is establishing closer partnerships with external bodies such as the Business Disability Forum, and collaborating on the Disability Standard benchmark as a tool to identify and implement best practice. Gary's advice for employee network leaders is: *"Be focused, be purposeful, but most of all - just do it!"*

It is important to grasp that every good head of a business - be they CEO, Entrepreneur, Permanent Secretary, Commissioner, Director, Principal etc. wants to have a reputation of being fair, and forward-thinking. Most recognise that diversity and inclusion makes good business sense and is deliberately encouraged. Who wants the inference of inequality or exclusion on their watch? No one does.

However, he or she doesn't have all the answers. In fact, they may not have even thought of the right questions or issues. They would naturally rely on the word and the work of the Human Resources Director, the Director of Inclusion or Head of Equality, who may be saying that everything is tickety-boo because they themselves may not be fully aware of the issues facing certain groups of staff. In addition, they might just de-prioritise or see particular issues pertaining to certain groups as a lower priority amidst other competing priorities. They may have provided opportunities for staff to engage but received a low response rate. So how do they find out what is really happening at the coalface? Bring in a consultant? Do yet another staff survey? Maybe.

I believe that staff networks can be part of this solution.

Staff networks can go a long way in providing an important intervention to assist organisations in fulfilling more than their legal responsibilities. Staff networks can cultivate a safe environment where permission is given to discuss some of those sensitive issues pertaining to a particular group.

Or as Peter Hall (Employers Network for Equality & Inclusion) puts it: *"...normalise the discussion."*

"Business leaders should be passionate about inclusiveness and start to see staff networks as internal think tanks to test things out and contribute to the inclusive agenda and the business goals." (Beth Clutterbuck, HSBC Bank)

Robert Smid (PwC) says that *"...diversity groups are more than support groups. They can help build a better brand for the organisation."*

Power Tip

Ensure that your house is in order and get your evidence together. Get some quick wins under your belt - things that you can shout about. Have you got your record of achievement to hand? Is it up to date? What were the outcomes? Gather and underline your evidence and make sure the right people see it and understand it.

Staff networks can share the experience of their members. In doing so, they can persuade management that being proactive in supporting diverse cultural realities of the communities of staff that make up the organisation and involving them in the decision process makes good business sense.

Are there issues affecting other minority groups? Why not work collaboratively with other staff networks to find some of the common challenges? There is power when different staff networks pull together to find a solution to a corporate problem. Dionne Campbell-Mark (Career Mentor) says: *"Identify synergies between your work and others' and work collaboratively to achieve results. The wider you spread your network, the greater the rewards and influence."*

One person who understands the importance of collaborative working among staff networks is Halil Huseyin. He is the Chair of the umbrella group Staff-support Associations Meeting Up Regularly And Interacting (S.A.M.U.R.A.I.). SAMURAI is the largest Police Diversity Forum in UK Policing, based in the Metropolitan Police Service (MPS). S.A.M.U.R.A.I. houses 19 staff networks and acts as the focal point between the staff networks and the wider MPS. Huseyin says:

"It is important to tease out the common themes emerging from the different staff networks and raise these with senior managers as a collective and collaborative voice. Staff networks (or Staff Support Associations as more commonly known within the MPS) are like the conscience of the organisation and therefore, we have to remain focused, and foster a harmonious relationship so that outcomes are improved for staff network members and the MPS as a whole."

Case Study: Black, Asian and Minority Ethnic Network (BAMENet), Department for Communities and Local Government (DCLG)

BAMEnet had become moribund after its first few years of existence and some members decided a fresh approach was needed. The staff network adopted clear strategic priorities linked to the Department's business plan, based on what it knew were members' chief concerns. Each priority was assigned clearly-defined actions, delivery dates and an individual to be responsible for it. BAMEnet used its relationships with senior management more effectively and purposefully worked in partnership with board members and senior colleagues at a strategic and operational level to influence DCLG's agenda. They highlighted the problems but also provided solutions. They worked collaboratively with HR to identify gaps in service provision, pulling together a powerful and inspirational range of events to help plug those gaps. Their activities were targeted at members but open to everyone to maximise the benefit. During the Department's restructuring, members used their skills and knowledge to devise and deliver a training course called the "Assessment Masterclass" which aimed to help members submit strong job applications. The course was so effective, that it was rolled out to the whole department. BAMEnet also demonstrated its ability to use their intelligence and external contacts to help shape internal policy. For example, immediately after the August riots in 2011, network members went to their affected communities with two aims:

(i) To advise affected businesses about the support available from central and local Government; and

(ii) To identify the barriers businesses were facing in getting back to normal trading. The information from the members proved invaluable to the policy team who were able to advise Ministers about the real issues affecting people on the ground and how to address them.

If you have a strong narrative, based on evidence that can help improve outcomes for your members, and ultimately, the overall health of the organisation, you need to talk about it. More importantly, you need others to talk about it.

Staff network Champion

A staff network Champion is someone who openly supports the staff network (some are akin to superheroes!). While they may not have any real super powers, they can be a powerful ally. Ideally, they should

be a senior manager because support at the highest level is crucial if the staff network is to be taken seriously (Dr Dianne Bebbington, Diversity Advisor). They don't have to be a member of your target group either. Please try not to be 'star-struck'. It is wise to ensure that there is a clear understanding about their role from the outset. Your Champion is your Champion because they listen, can carry a message, and are willing to lend the weight of their leadership to the staff network. Whether you choose your Champion or your Champion was appointed to your staff network, it is important that this person has an understanding of what it is you are trying to do and advocates your work. However, they are not experts in your experience so you will need to help populate their knowledge in this area.

The Champion should be vocal about the achievements of the staff network (so ensure that you have noted these). They are there to tell their circle of influence about your work and how it benefits the organisation. The Champion can reach parts of the business that you might not be able to, so be clear about the messages you need them to convey. The staff network should ideally take the lead in this relationship - not the Champion. When necessary, give them the lines to take. Hold each other accountable through regular and focused meetings.

Power Thought: Definition of a Champion

"A person who vigorously supports or defends a person or cause."

Other words synonymous with Champion: advocate, proponent, promoter, torchbearer, protector, upholder, backer, exponent, patron, sponsor.

In addition, the Champion should be prepared to:

- Participate at events (give them key messages/announcements).
- Visibly endorse participation in the staff network.
- Hold scheduled meetings with the staff network.
- Champion the group amongst his/her peers.

- Brief the staff network committee on issues arising that could affect members.
- Help to align staff networks with mainstream functions and services.

Benefit of being a Champion:

- Useful insight into staff perceptions of what is happening on the ground.
- Grounded awareness of how policies and practices impact staff.
- Increased knowledge and capacity to understand diversity issues.
- In a better position to proactively respond to changes.
- Provide a conduit and sounding board to innovative solutions identified to corporate challenges.
- Identify the talent within the organisation.

"As a diversity champion it is a huge help for me to have a lively and active staff network to engage with, provide ideas and feedback and challenge where it's due."

(Steve Gooding, Race & Religion Diversity Champion, Dept. for Transport)

Possible outcomes:

- Raise awareness of the staff network and some of the issues faced by certain groups of staff.
- Allocation of reasonable resources.
- Provision of facility time for staff to participate in staff network activities (sends clear message to those managers who might trivialise the work of staff networks).
- Recognition and reward of staff network contribution.

The relationship between the staff network and the Champion is key if you want to work with or change perceptions in the organisation.

Consider the existing rapport that the staff network has with other key players in the business. If a member of the staff network has already established a solid connection with someone of influence, tap into that.

Involving the right people to represent the staff network in dealings with senior managers is legacy mentality. It doesn't always have to be the Chair/ Vice Chair etc. who meet with the senior people.

Jennifer Smith, Circle Housing says:

> *"Our diversity networks have found benefits in hosting meetings in the different partner organisations as well as being able to make new contacts at all levels in the organisation. The network Chairs and key members regularly have contact with the Executive team, in formal and informal settings."*

Other things to take into account when building the relationship with senior managers:

- Is the staff network a trusted and reliable source of information? Have you provided information that proved correct and useful? Can managers trust your intelligence to be accurate? Here's a quote from a former Chair of a BAME staff network: *"One of the biggest compliments I received was when the head of the company said to me that he always made sure he had his ducks in a row whenever we met."*

  Why? Because this Chair attended the meetings armed with evidence and intelligence that was useful to the Champion. When asked about the rationale behind her approach, the Chair said: *"I have a demanding day job and therefore my time is precious. I go armed with my evidence. You can't argue with evidence. Flannel belongs in the bathroom, not the boardroom."*

- The successes of the staff network - what credits do you have to your name? What have you achieved and what were the outcomes? What are members saying about your work? What is your Champion saying?

- Whenever you meet with senior managers, park your grade at the door. The staff network has a voice - a very powerful voice. View your staff network as a valuable asset. This is your leverage - you can reach parts senior managers cannot reach. You are there to remind management that there are challenges and issues that affect the organisation but you are there to help provide solutions to some of those challenges so that the workplace is inclusive, employees are engaged and business goals are achieved.

- Be aware of what it is you would like them to do – put yourself in their shoes and offer workable solutions that are within their power to take forward.

Power Advice:

If you're in a non-managerial role/grade, do not allow your junior or administrative status to dictate how you behave as a Chair. If you're meeting with a CEO of an organisation, remember that you are the 'CEO' of the staff network and act accordingly with courtesy, charm and grace, but be assertive and confident. It's the **4G** effect:

1) **G**et your facts straight

2) **G**ather your evidence

3) **G**arner your questions/challenges

4) **G**enerously offer solutions

How you conduct yourself in the staff network will have a direct impact on how you are seen outside the staff network.

Benefits to the organisation

A healthy working relationship between the staff network and managers can lead to a number of benefits:

- Staff are developed by improving their knowledge of the business and wider social issues.
- Positive investment in members leads to better motivated staff.
- Members feel empowered to seek out opportunities to grow and be ambitious.

- Involvement in the staff network demonstrates a commitment to equality, valuing diversity and emulating inclusion.
- The staff network is a valuable business resource, influencing decision-making by providing timely and effective feedback.
- Helps to build trust and supports employee engagement.
- Lower absenteeism rates.

Benefits to the staff network

- Gains respect and influence.
- Becomes a trusted source of information.
- Gives members a staff network to be proud of which could trigger a desire to get more involved.
- Skills are developed and opportunities created.
- Confidence is boosted.
- Vehicle for creating positive change benefiting members.

Chapter summary

The key to a fruitful relationship between the staff network and management is transparency, trust, collaboration and effective communication. Be open about what you are doing and why. Be prepared to work with people outside the staff network to achieve your outcome. Exploit every opportunity to share the good news of the staff network.

Be prepared to manage upward to move the staff network forward.

CHAPTER NINE:
SUCCESSION PLANNING

"Good people can make poor systems work, poor people can make good systems fail."
(Lorraine Thomas, Department of Health)

Throughout this book, I've mentioned the importance of having a legacy mentality and therefore, I wanted to address the issue of succession planning. Many staff networks struggle with this so I hope that this chapter will offer some clarification and help staff networks understand the benefits of putting something in place to secure its future.

Unfortunately, too many staff network leaders wait until they are either burnt out, about to leave the organisation, or totally fed up with the staff network before they start to consider who to hand over to. That is not succession planning; that's poor planning. They somehow feel that the right person will mysteriously appear and lead the staff network. That, my friend, is also not succession planning; that's wishful thinking! Succession planning should be a first-thought and not an after-thought.

What is Succession Planning?

According to the CIPD, succession planning may be broadly defined as a process for identifying and developing potential future leaders, as well as individuals to fill other business-critical positions, either in the short- or the long-term. In addition to training and development activities, succession planning programmes typically include the provision of practical, tailored work experience that will be relevant for future key roles.

Power Anecdote:

I recall having a conversation with someone about succession planning for the staff network and wanted to know how the organisation handled succession planning generally. During a period when a large tranche of people were leaving the organisation due to redundancy, I asked a senior HR manager this question. He was of the opinion that if people wanted to "take the money and run", who was he to stop them? However, my concern was not just the fact that people were leaving but they were taking their knowledge, their experience, their contacts, their relationships, everything with them. There was no plan in place to capture that bank of information. No plan at all.

This is what sometimes happens in staff networks. Not having a succession plan is a bit like wanting to run in a relay race with no idea who you're passing the baton to or how you're going to pass it. The person holding the baton has the responsibility of handing it to the next runner at the right time. How they hand over the baton will determine whether the next runner gets a good grip or drops it. For a successful baton exchange, the runners will set aside a period where they train together, and agree when and how the baton should be passed on. As one person comes to the end of their leg, the next person starts theirs. Both will run their leg to the best of their ability to help the team achieve the overarching aim - winning the race. It's the same with a staff network.

Successful succession planning is vital to sustain the life of a staff network, and yet it is rare to find a staff network that does it well.

One Chair opined that *"...succession planning is a conundrum."* Perhaps the problem is the mindset. As well as considering what the staff network needs now, succession planning should be steering you to think about what the staff network needs in the future.

Issues around succession planning

I have heard many Chairs of staff networks say things like: *"Yeah, I have a vice-chair but I just don't think they are ready."* or: *"I want to step down but who will take it over? I can't just leave it, can I?"* Both statements may be quite valid but do they really help to foster the right frame of mind for succession planning?

Chairs also cited the following issues that could hinder effectively implementing a succession planning strategy:

- Concern regarding the continuation of the work/legacy of the staff network;
- High turnover of committee team makes it difficult;
- Lack of training and support on succession planning for staff networks;
- Perception about the staff network is an issue (both from members and wider organisation);
- 'Founders' Syndrome' impedes succession planning;
- Lack of capacity building;
- Not attracting the right people.

Possible solutions

Identify and inspire the right Chair:

- It might be worth thinking about how to help people prepare to lead a staff network. Understand and accept that people may not have all the qualities initially and will need time to grow into the role. So incumbent Chairs need to purposefully look out for individuals and inspire them to get involved. You could offer to mentor them or expose them to the opportunities you have, e.g. key meetings with senior managers, include it as an objective for their performance appraisal/personal development plan, inform them of the skills they will learn from the experience and how these could be useful in the future.

Strong Terms of Reference (ToR):

- The ToR should cover length of tenure which should help to prevent maladies such as Founders' Syndrome;
- The ToR should also be independently ratified to establish transparent governance and encourage member engagement.

Specific action for staff networks:

- Personal Capacity – learn how to build capacity of the Chairs/leaders (and other management team members) to take forward actions that deliver outcomes.
- Consider whether there is a perception about the staff network that needs to change (check your brand).
- Think about how to educate members to understand that involvement in staff networks can be a corporate objective and an opportunity to strengthen competencies and skills.
- Keep your eyes open and be prepared to offer a range of development opportunities such as mentoring, coaching, leading action learning sets, stretching projects (e.g. leading a work programme).

Action for organisations:

- A need to understand how to reap staff network dividends.
- Consider holding staff networks to account for their contribution to the business.
- Invest in capacity building.
- Develop and/or share the in-house succession planning model.
- Remember that hundreds of thousands of pounds are awarded in individual employment tribunals every year to people who have been discriminated against in work.
- Have an external measure of success to spur motivation e.g. benchmarking, awards, targets.

Chapter summary

There are no hard and fast rules to succession planning for staff networks, but having a legacy mentality is a good place to start. I hope the following serves as a useful reminder:

Identify	Purposely look out for individuals
Inspire	Motivate them to get involved
Invest	Encourage and support them
Inaugurate	Put them in place (include induction/handover)

Keeping these at the front of your mind should help to ensure that succession planning is not an afterthought.

CHAPTER TEN:
DEAR CHAIR

"Those who water, will always be watered."
(The Bible, Proverbs 11:25)

This chapter is specifically aimed at Chairs (or potential Chairs) and is written in the style of a letter. I wanted Chairs to have something to refer to on those days when some encouragement is required.

Dear Chair,

Firstly, congratulations on taking up the post as Chair of your staff network. You are in a wonderful position to be a catalyst for change. "Me?" Yes, you. Anything that the staff network does to help improve the working environment for members of its target group, and to help the employer appreciate difference, *is* a positive change. Like any leadership position, leading a staff network is not an easy task and there may be times when you experience one or more of the following:

Frustation	Crisis of Confidence	Insecure	Sense of Purpose	Fed-Up
Doubtful	Tearful	Confused	Worried	Out of Your Depth
Excited	Discouraged	Discombobulated	Emotional	Weak
Strong	In Control	Jealous	Driven	Happy

I can tell you that if you experience one or more of these emotions or moods, then that is quite normal. You are not alone. Leading a staff network is not an easy role. However, it can be extremely rewarding and enjoyable. So here is some advice from the heart to encourage and inspire you as you lead.

- Allow yourself to grow into your role. If you are a new Chair, sometimes there is a tussle between trying to emulate the former Chair (if they were effective and dynamic), and making your mark.

- Be uncommonly curious about your own personal development during your time as Chair. Yes, you need to deliver and achieve for the staff network but think about what skills/knowledge you want to develop personally.

- Be a Chair of **I.C.E.** No, I don't mean be stone-cold but rather:
  Integrity - say what you mean, mean what you say.
  Character - not to be confused with reputation. Abraham Lincoln said: "*Character is like a tree and reputation is like its shadow. The shadow is what we think of it; the tree is the real thing.*" Be genuine.
  Excellence - do what you can to the <u>best</u> of your ability for the best of the staff network.

- Take control of your time. In addition to running the staff network, you probably have a 'day' job, and other personal responsibilities (e.g. family, studying, volunteering etc.). If you haven't done so already, negotiate time for your staff network duties. But you will still need to be creative in how you use your time. Travelling time is great to catch up on emails, review papers etc. Remember, you don't have to do everything - master the art of mindful delegation.

- Ensure you have a good support system in place. This is team 'YOU [insert your name]' (e.g. Team Charlie). Team 'YOU' should comprise people you trust and in whose opinion you hold confidence. Team 'YOU' will be people who value you and will offer you constructive feedback because they want the best for you, and from you. They will be people who can encourage you, who will challenge you, who will make you laugh, who will coach you, or who will just listen to you sounding off. Every Chair needs their own team; their inner circle.

- Remember to prioritise "us" over "me" - be inclusive, collaborative and practice what you preach.
- Be generous and specific in your praise, in your encouragement and with your attention. Share credit.
- Take note of these 'Rules of Leadership' (Courtesy of Perry Noble and Benjamin Conway):

  1) Not everyone will like you.

  2) It is not your goal for everyone to like you.

  3) The better you lead, the more people may not like you.

- Do not become complacent and take your role for granted. There is a fantastic Jamaican Patois phrase that says: *"Wanti wanti cyan getti getti and getti getti nuh want it"* (literal word for word translation: want it want it can't get it and get it get it don't want it). There are people who would love to lead a staff network but, for whatever reason, are unable to. Then, there are others who are in the position but don't appreciate it and take things for granted. The gist is: *be thankful and embrace what you have because there are always people who would exchange places with you in an instant.*

- Take a look at the 'qualities' below. I encourage you to try and arm yourself with as many of these as possible. They will prove invaluable both during your tenure as Chair and beyond.

Well-grounded	Strategic Thinker	Solution Focussed	Values Driven	Able to Share Success
Drive a Compelling Narrative	Generous	Common Sense Drive	Resilient (Rhino-hide)	Opportunity Hunter
Business Focussed	Energy & Authenticity	Communication Skills	Lead with Grace	Personal Mastery
Planning Skills	Pragmatic	Analytical	Credible & Authoritative	Forward Thinking

- Before you leave your role as Chair, take the time to complete a 'due diligence' handover checklist. Lorraine Thomas (former Chair of the Equality Matters staff network at the Department of Health) found this a really useful exercise. The checklist is a great way of helping the incumbent Chair to ensure that the incoming Chair has no surprises (and it's a really nice thing to do). She devised a template which helped her accurately outline the key issues for her successor. *(See table 1 on the following page.)*

- Don't be afraid to rule with your head *and* your heart because:

Head	**Integrity** **Competencies:** • Acting consistently with principles, values and beliefs (walking the talk) • Telling the truth • Standing up for what is right • Keeping promises **Results in:** **Trust**	**Responsibility** **Competencies:** • Taking responsibility for personal choices • Admitting mistakes and failures • Embracing responsibilities for serving others - "leave the world a better place" **Results in:** **Inspiration**
Heart	**Forgiveness** **Competencies:** • Ability to let go of one's mistakes • Ability to let go of others' mistakes **Results in:** **Innovation**	**Compassion** **Competencies:** • Actively caring for others **Results in:** **Retention**

(Table courtesy of Nitin Kalra, PeopleStrong)

Finally:

✓ Focus on delivering outcomes.
✓ Deliberately develop yourself.
✓ Be determined to make a change.
✓ Have fun and enjoy the ride.

All the best.

Cherron

Table 1 - Due Diligence Table

Area	Required for a maturing network	Details to consider	Proposed actions to continue	Who	Reference Docs
Rationale for Network	• Staff Network (SN) aims are to support organisation (ORG) in meeting its Equality Act (EA) 2010 and more specifically diversity responsibilities – this provides the necessary evidence for the SN and wider stakeholders	• Indicative structure developed along with aims, objectives and priorities • Strapline retains focus on supporting ORG so SN activity can be seen as a corporate activity	• Develop workable operating model – SN themes better aligned to wider ORG priority descriptors	• Chair • Thematic leads	• Equality Act 2010 • EA 2010 Public Sector Equality Duty

Other areas could include: Direction Setting, Work Planning, Relationship with Senior Officials/Champions, Reporting, Secretariat, Communication, Policy, Learning and Capability, Compliance and Information.

CONCLUSION

"...and while the water is stirring,
I will step into the pool."
(Sojourner Truth)

Let's us go back to the beginning of this journey. Two years and three months after I sat in that conference room in December 2009, I was there again. This time, I was not annoyed or frustrated; but proud. I stood on a podium facing a full room of enthusiastic network members and supporters waiting for me to give my farewell speech. My tenure had come to an end. I had run my race and it was time for the incoming management team to run theirs. After an induction and handover period, they were ready and waiting to take the baton. Through our achievements, outcomes and success, our staff network had created a great stir and it was the moment for others to step into the pool.

My final piece of advice is to remember the 10 Cs:

1. **Consider** decisions as if you were the employer.

2. **Challenges** develop and strengthen staff networks (overcome them).

3. **Capacity** building is integral to your mission.

4. **Contribute** your best at all times.

5. **Create reciprocity and clearly communicate** your goals.

6. **Connect** with members, allies and others in the organisation.

7. **Complacency** and apathy are saboteurs.

8. Commit to reviewing the staff network - sustainability mentality.

9. Celebrate your successes and achievements (and share credit).

10. Choose to invest in things that are right and you will reap a dividend of the right things.

When you do these 10 things well, your staff network may enjoy the following outcomes (and more):

- Active championing by senior management.
- Facility time for members to participate in meetings and activities.
- Allocation of resources.
- Roles and work shared amongst group members, which is formally recognised and rewarded by the employer.
- Realistic and achievable objectives, reviewed periodically.
- Transparent reporting structures and feedback mechanisms and opportunities to inform the change process.
- Strategies to inform and involve staff and raise awareness of a staff network within the organisation e.g. induction days, recruitment material.
- Support from those areas that deal with people matters (i.e. Equality & Diversity, Trade Unions, Human Resources, senior managers).
- A business with a well-developed culture of staff consultation and engagement.

I have learnt so much from my involvement in staff networks and I wanted to pay this forward.

After reading this book, I hope your staff network will be in a position where:

- Members feel supported, motivated, challenged, empowered and encouraged.
- Through your insight and collective intelligence, managers acknowledge that things could be improved and commit to taking action.

- Your networks and connections prove invaluable.
- In the absence of position power, your members develop their personal power to create change for themselves and the organisation.
- In sharing my knowledge and experience, I hope that I can help staff networks adopt the right mindset and establish a solid foundation to be successful and make a difference to their members and the business.

Staff networks - you have the **P.O.W.E.R.**

"The most common way people give up their power, is by thinking they don't have any."
(Alice Walker)

RESOURCES

Remember

1 • The right mindset and a solid foundation are essential for a successful staff network

2 • Think carefully about your plan and execute with purpose (UNDER PROMISE, OVER DELIVER)

3 • Work collaboratively using your members, your allies and your Champion to achieve your goals

4 • Develop a productive relationship with senior management and share your insight

5 • A succession plan is crucial to the sustainability and legacy of the staff network

6 • Focus on delivering outcomes, deliberately develop yourself, be determined to make a change, and have fun

Terms of Reference: Template 1

[NAME OF STAFF NETWORK]

Terms of Reference

Purpose

- The purpose of the NAME OF STAFF NETWORK is to give DIVERSITY GROUP staff a means of raising collective issues in relation to their employment and provide a means for the ORGANISATION to consult on employment policies and practices.
- In addition, the staff network will consult on changing the culture of ORGANISATION and provide views on how it can best deliver services to the DIVERSITY GROUP community.

Objectives

- Provide a means of raising work-related issues collectively and in partnership with other staff forums.
- Provide an opportunity to meet with colleagues, share ideas and network in a safe environment.
- The STAFF NETWORK will work in partnership with the other forums and its aim is helping ORGANISATION to achieve equality and diversity across all strands.
- To assist managers to identify and remove barriers to improve the recruitment and retention of DIVERSITY GROUP staff.
- To act as a critical friend to inform managers decision-making.
- To consider and comment upon employment issues related to DIVERSITY GROUP staff referred to the STAFF NETWORK by the Corporate Equalities Team/HR.
- To contribute to the development and implementation of the ORGANISATIONS DIVERSITY/INCLUSION STRATEGY and the forthcoming work around EQUALITY AREA as well as issues specific to DIVERSITY GROUP.
- To work with the ORGANISATION and all staff to ensure that everyone has equal access to services, regardless of age, disability, race, gender, religion or belief and sexual orientation.

Membership

- All ORGANISATION staff, including interim and agency staff, who identify with being DIVERSITY GROUP. Membership is also extended to staff, partners and colleagues who are interested in learning about and supporting issues in the DIVERSITY GROUP community.

- There is no restriction on numbers of staff at this STAFF NETWORK. Both Trade Union and Non Trade Union Members are welcome. Staff Diversity Forums are led by the ORGANISATION.

- The STAFF NETWORK will elect a Chair, co-chair and minute taker/secretary who will be responsible for servicing these meetings. Other roles may be added as and when necessary.

Reporting Lines and Management Arrangements

- Members of the STAFF NETWORK will nominate a chair, co-chair and minute taker.

- Minutes of the meetings will be published on the intranet. The Chair of the STAFF NETWORK will update CORPORATE EQUALITIES/DIVERSITY TEAM on discussions and report any actions or progress on a quarterly basis.

- Any actions that need to be taken by the ORGANISATION which is agreed by the STAFF NETWORK will be directed to the relevant senior managers and to the CORPORATE EQUALITIES by the Chair of the STAFF NETWORK.

- CORPORATE EQUALITIES will review the STAFF NETWORK'S business plan and look at the purpose of the STAFF NETWORK annually in conjunction with the STAFF NETWORK.

Meetings

- STAFF NETWORK will meet on at least a quarterly basis but may meet more frequently if necessary.

Facilities

- The attendance of employee representatives on the STAFF NETWORK is conditional upon agreement from line managers and will be subject to the needs of their service. However, managers will be encouraged to make it easier for staff to attend the STAFF NETWORK.
- Members of the STAFF NETWORK will be allowed X hours paid to attend the meetings plus travel time. Reasonable time to consult other members of staff and conduct research requested by the STAFF NETWORK will be considered by line managers in conjunction with the Chair.
- The STAFF NETWORK will receive an annual budget subject to agreement of CORPORATE EQUALITIES/DIVERSITY TEAM. The budget will be used for running costs and to address issues identified by the STAFF NETWORK.

Further information

- Queries should be referred to Chair and/or co-chair of the STAFF NETWORK, and by email at EMAIL ADDRESS.
- See our page on the intranet/internet at LINK for details about forthcoming events and dates of our meetings.

Terms of Reference: Template 2

THE GREEN-EYED MANAGERS & STAFF (GEMS) NETWORK TERMS OF REFERENCE AND GOVERNANCE ARRANGEMENTS

It is important to have appropriate guidance in place to ensure that the GEMS operates in a fair and transparent way so that the legacy of its core aims lives on. The purpose of this document is to provide a clear outline of how to manage the network so that it continues to be a vanguard in helping improve outcomes for GEMS within the organisation and lead the way in giving people opportunities to excel.

Aim

The GEMS exists to:

1. Provide GREEN-EYED staff with a voice through empowerment and support;
2. Represent the interests of GREEN-EYED staff within the organisation; and
3. Work with senior management to build an organisation where equity and equality of opportunities exists for all.

How will we do this?

GEMS will:

- Work with HR and other parts of the business to ensure that formal policies and practices do not adversely impact GREEN-EYED staff.;
- Provide our members with a voice by working with colleagues to progress the issues that impact on and concern our members;
- Help to ensure that equality and diversity issues continue to be promoted and embedded within the organisation's core values and their behaviour is consistent with this; and
- Give people a chance to shine within the network by providing opportunities for members to get involved in activities, events etc.

Membership

GEMs is open to anyone who supports our aims and is especially targeted at those within the organisation's workforce who either identify as belonging to or relating to those with GREEN EYES.

Meetings

Members will meet every three months. A schedule for meetings will be supplied by the management team. The management team to meet at least once a month.

Agenda

Members shall be able to ask that any item be placed on the agenda seven days before the date of the meeting. The Agenda for the meetings shall be coordinated by the Business Secretary/Chair. A note of the meeting should be circulated within 14 working days of the meeting.

Management Team

The management team will be elected from the membership to support the delivery of the aims. The management team shall be a core minimum of six people and a maximum of ten at the discretion of the management team.

The positions are:

Chair whose responsibilities will include (but are not limited to):

- Preparation of agendas for meetings.
- Facilitation of meetings.
- Providing the membership with regular updates on progress.
- Holding regular meetings with GEMs' Champion (who can have a different eye colour).
- Updating critical friends regularly.

Deputy Chair whose responsibilities will include (but are not limited to):

- Assisting the Chair in the delivery of aims.

- In the event that the Chair is temporarily unable to meet his or her responsibilities, wherever possible the Deputy Chair will act on behalf of the Chair.

Business Secretary whose responsibilities will include (but are not limited to):

- Liaising with the Chair to arrange meetings.
- Taking and disseminating notes of meetings.
- Advising members of upcoming meetings.

Communications Officer whose responsibilities will include (but are not limited to):

- Editor-in-chief of the quarterly GEMS Newsletter.
- Ensuring information about the GEMS is placed on the intranet and is updated regularly.
- Ensuring consistency of communication style and GEMs messaging.

Membership Liaison Officer whose responsibilities will include (but are not limited to):

- Actively recruiting members.
- Liaising and provide development support for members.
- Maintaining up-to-date membership lists including statistics.
- Taking the lead on the skills exchange and buddy programmes.

Social Secretary whose responsibilities will include (but are not limited to):

- Taking the lead in informing members of various social activities (internal and external).
- Providing some support to the business secretary.
- Advising members of upcoming meetings.

Up to four people can be co-opted to join the management team to undertake specific projects. Co-options should be for a minimum of six months and a maximum of 18 months (with reviews at six monthly intervals). This enables the management team to widen its skills base from time to time and also gives opportunities to people in GEMS to develop their skills. The management team may at any time form task and finish working teams, drawn from the membership to work on, and report to members on issues that affect GREEN-EYED staff.

Ending the Appointment of a Management Team member

If the management team and elected members feel that a fellow elected member is not fulfilling their duties, there is a process to democratically remove them. In particular, but without limitation, the appointment is also subject to termination by the management team where an appointee:

a) Has by their actions, brought, or is likely to bring, the staff network into disrepute; and

b) When their behaviour adversely impacts the smooth running of management team business (outputs and outcomes).

It is the responsibility of the elected members and management team to have an informal conversation with the elected member to identify where they are not fulfilling their role and give them the opportunity to either increase engagement or step down from their role. If a solution is not reached or the situation fails to improve over a reasonable period of time, the management team may call on someone to mediate the situation. If both steps have been taken and are unsuccessful, the management team and the elected members have the right to vote on whether the person should continue on the management team. A two-thirds majority must be reached in order for an elected member to be removed from the committee. If a vacancy arises following the vote, elections for the role will be held within 30 working days.

Decision Making

Decisions on the administration of the staff network shall be taken by the management team on the basis of a simple majority voting. For decisions to be taken by the management team, there must be a quorum. Critical issues for the network should be put to the full membership and these will be decided on the basis of simple majority voting. Voting may be carried out by a show of hands at a formal meeting, electronically, in writing or in any way the management team deems fit.

Length of Service

GEMS will provide development opportunities for its GREEN-EYED membership. To create these opportunities and maintain a fresh outlook:

- The term of the management team shall be for two years starting in April of the election year.
- Existing members who have been on the management team for longer than two years should step down and be replaced.

Elections

All members are eligible to stand for election to the management team and elections shall be carried out by means of a simple majority decision by members.

- The elections shall be held during the months of January and February in an election year and the management team will ensure that the necessary arrangements are in place for a new management team to be appointed by the end of April in any election year.
- For the sake of openness and transparency, an independent adjudicator should be appointed to oversee the proceedings for the elections.
- The new management team shall take up its responsibilities from April. It will be the responsibility of the new management team to draft a new business plan and objectives for the new financial year.
- Members will be notified of the election and given 20 working days to vote by means of a postal or electronic ballot.
- Nominations for the management team should not be a surprise to the nominee. Therefore all nominations should be agreed with the nominee in advance.

- In the event of a tie for the final place(s), the other successful management team members will have the casting vote to settle the issue.

Confidentiality

- Members are not under any obligation to declare any information about themselves that they do not wish to share.
- The group will operate a 'safe space' approach to meetings and treat all network members with dignity and respect.
- Records of meetings will be kept, but names will not be included on notes or minutes that will be circulated outside the group membership.

Monitoring, Evaluation and Reporting

The management team will prepare an internal business plan for the forthcoming financial year and update it annually (or more frequently if need be). The business plan should:

a) Set objectives, covering GEMs operation, for the forthcoming financial year against which its performance can be readily evaluated and reported on in the corresponding Annual Report;

b) Give key information on future expenditure proposals and objectives, highlighting - where appropriate - significant changes from the previous year; and

c) Reflect relevant decisions on policy and resources.

The management team will report on its activities at every meeting of the full membership and once a year produce a written account (Annual Report) of its activities.

Review of Governance Arrangements

These arrangements will be reviewed by each in coming management team and any changes recommended to the membership.

Sample letter in support of staff networks

From: HR Director

To: All Managers

We are committed to ensure all staff - whatever their background, current role or career path - can improve their job satisfaction and contribution to the organisation year-on-year.

To facilitate this, HR supports the work of staff networks. Engaging with staff and supporting our staff networks remains a priority. This organisation is fortunate to have a number of staff networks and I'm writing to ask you to actively encourage your staff to support them and attend events.

As well as providing an opportunity for under-represented or vulnerable staff to be part of a forum where their voice can be heard, staff networks not only empower staff but provide them with important support.

Using our staff networks is an important part of our engagement strategy.

Wall of Inspiration

Good staff networks exist for the betterment of their members but require good volunteers to ensure they meet their needs.
(Jerome Williams)

Powerful networks strive to engage all members to encourage, support and inspire each other to offer their best!
(Rob Neil)

Push through personal gain for the staff network's gain.
(Dionne Campbell-Mark)

Belt up and get ready for the ride!
(Diane Greenidge)

Be as transparent as you possibly can.
(Halil Huseyin)

Dare to succeed. You can do more than you think you can!
(Peter Hall)

Every staff network member is a piece of the jigsaw. Join and complete the picture!
(Paul Deemer)

A good chair will be a role model to members of the network and won't attempt to overstay their tenure unless invited/agreed by members.
(Barbara Lindsay MBE)

Support
Knowledge
Inspiration
Listening, and
Learning.
Remember, all it takes is S.K.I.L.L.
(Roianne Nedd)

For staff networks to be heard, senior leaders in their organisation need to listen.
(Claire Herbert)

Be focused, be purposeful, but most of all - just do it!
(Gary Denton)

Listen and read to learn from others' mistakes...but be sure not to forget that context is important. What was true for them may not be true for your situation and should not stop you from living your dreams.
(David Onigbanjo)

REFERENCES

- Bebbington. D. (2007). Diversity Champions. Engage 12(Q4), p.13.

- Belbin Associates: www.belbin.com

- Blanchard. K. (2010). Perspectives: Building Trust.

- Chartered Institute of Personnel and Development. (2013). Megatrends: Are organisations losing the trust of their workers?

- Childs, J. B. (1992). Constructive disputing: The ramifications of African-American caucuses for today's organizations. Studies in Law, Politics, and Society, 1992, *12*, 177-197.

- Chua, C. (2014). Personal Excellence. Eight Helpful Ways to Deal with Critical People. http://personalexcellence.co/

- Confederation of British Industry and Trade Union Congress (2008). Talent Not Tokenism: The Business Benefits of Workforce Diversity

- Department for Energy and Climate Change. (2012). Equality, Diversity and Inclusion Strategy 2012-2015

- Douglas, P. A. (2008). Affinity Groups: Catalyst for Inclusive Organisations. Employment Relations Today, 11-18. doi:10.1002/ert.20171

- Fligstein, N. (1997). Social skill and institutional theory. American Behavioural Scientist, 40(4), 397-405.

- Friedman, R. A. (1999). Employee Network Groups: Self-Help Strategy for Women and Minorities. Performance Improvement Quarterly, 12(1), 148-163.

- Friedman, R. A., and Bogar, E. (2012). Trends in Corporate Policy Development for Employee Network Groups. Nashville: Owen Graduate School of Management- Vanderbilt University.

- Friedman, R., Kane, M., & Cornfield, D. B. (1998). Social Support and Career Optimism: Examining the Effectiveness of Network Groups Among Black Managers. Human Relations, 51(9), 1155-1177.

- Friedman, R.A., and Craig, K.M. (2004). Predicting Joining and Participating in Minority Employee Network Groups. Industrial Relations: A Journal of Economy and Society: Volume 43, Issue 4, pages 793–816.

- Gaule, S., and Box, M. (2008). Making the case for Staff Networks. Leadership Foundation in Higher Education, In Practice: Issue 15

- Gaule, S., and Box, M. (2008). Staff Networks: A guide to setting up sustainable and effective employee network groups in higher education institutes. Liverpool John Moores University.

- (The) Health Foundation. (2014). Effective Networks for Improvement http://www.health.org.uk/publications/effective-networks-for-improvement/

- Ibarra, H. (1993). Personal networks of women and minorities in management: A conceptual framework. Academy of Management Review, 18(1), 56–87.

- Jayne, M. A., and Dipboye, R. L. (2000). Leveraging Diversity to Improve Business Performance: Research Findings and Recommendations for Organisations. Human Resource Management, 43(4), 409-424. doi:10.1002/hrm.20033

- Johnson, S. (2002). Who Moved My Cheese?. Putnam

- Katz, N., Lazer, D., and Arrow H (2004). Network Theory and Small Groups. Small Group Research 35: 307-332

- Klandermans, B. (1986). Psychology and Trade Union Participation: Joining, Acting, and Quitting. Journal of Occupational Psychology 59:198–204.

- Jaferi, T (2014). "Microaggressions": Trendy buzz-word or something to think about?. Turner Consulting Group

- http://turnerconsultinggroup.weebly.com/blog-thamina-jaferi

- Lee, H. (1960). To Kill a Mockingbird

- Liverpool Primary Care Trust and Liverpool Community Health NHS Trust. Guidance on Staff Networks: Embracing Diversity and Promoting Equality of Opportunity

- Patterson, K., Grenny, J., McMillan, R., Switzler, A. (2012). Crucial Conversations. McGraw-Hill

- Purcell, J and Hall, M. (2012). Voice and Participation in the Modern Workplace: Challenges and Prospects, discussion paper (Advisory, Conciliation & Arbitration Service)

- Reynolds, L. (2014). 21st Century Leader. www.21stcenturyleader.co.uk

- Sawyer, J B. (2012). Social Ties and Authentic Deployment of Social Identity In the Workplace: How Employee Resource Groups serve the interests of minorities and the organizations for which they work. Vanderbilt Peabody College

- Sisson, K et al (1997). New Forms of Work Organisation: Can Europe Realise its Potential? (European Foundation for the Improvement of Living & Working Conditions)

- Sweeney, E. (2014) Making Work Better - An Agenda for Government: An independent inquiry into the world of work (The Smith Institute)

- Syedain, H. (2012). Workplace diversity. People Management. 24 August. with permission of the Chartered Institute of Personnel and Development.

- Subeliani, D. and Tsogas, G. (2005). Managing diversity in the Netherlands: a case study of Rabobank. International Journal of Human Resource Management, Vol. 16, No.5 May; pp 831-851.

- Willacy, K. The Difference is You (DIY). Equality Matters. http://www.equality-matters.co.uk/

- All quotes from brainyquote.com, thinkexist.com, leadershipnow.com, quotery.com

Further Reading

- *Consiglieri - Leading from the Shadows*: Richard Hytner (Profile Books, 2014)

- *Crucial Conversations*: Kerry Patterson, Joseph Grenny, Ron McMillan, Al Switzler (McGraw-Hill, 2012)

- *Who Moved My Cheese?*: Spencer Johnson (Putnam, 2002)